THE WOMEN'S MOVEMENT

AND THE RISE OF FEMINISM

By Nicole Horning

Portions of this book originally appeared in *The Women's Movement* by Don Nardo.

LUCENT
PRESS

Published in 2019 by
Lucent Press, an Imprint of Greenhaven Publishing, LLC
353 3rd Avenue
Suite 255
New York, NY 10010

Designer: Deanna Paternostro
Editor: Nicole Horning

Library of Congress Cataloging-in-Publication Data

Names: Horning, Nicole, author.
Title: The women's movement and the rise of feminism / Nicole Horning.
Description: New York : Lucent Press, [2019] | Series: World history |
  Includes bibliographical references and index.
Identifiers: LCCN 2018004061 (print) | LCCN 2018002342 (ebook) | ISBN
  9781534563773 (eBook) | ISBN 9781534563766 (library bound book) | ISBN
  9781534563780 (pbk. book)
Subjects: LCSH: Feminism—United States—History. | Feminism—History.
Classification: LCC HQ1410 (print) | LCC HQ1410 .H67 2019 (ebook) | DDC
  305.420973—dc23
LC record available at https://lccn.loc.gov/2018004061

Printed in the United States of America

CPSIA compliance information: Batch #BS18KL: For further information contact Greenhaven Publishing LLC, New York, New York at 1-844-317-7404.

Please visit our website, www.greenhavenpublishing.com. For a free color catalog of all our high-quality books, call toll free 1-844-317-7404 or fax 1-844-317-7405.

Contents

Foreword

History books are often filled with names and dates—words and numbers for students to memorize for a test and forget once they move on to another class. However, what history books should be filled with are great stories, because the history of our world is filled with great stories. Love, death, violence, heroism, and betrayal are not just themes found in novels and movie scripts. They are often the driving forces behind major historical events.

When told in a compelling way, fact is often far more interesting—and sometimes far more unbelievable—than fiction. World history is filled with more drama than the best television shows, and all of it really happened. As readers discover the incredible truth behind the triumphs and tragedies that have impacted the world since ancient times, they also come to understand that everything is connected. Historical events do not exist in a vacuum. The stories that shaped world history continue to shape the present and will undoubtedly shape the future.

The titles in this series aim to provide readers with a comprehensive understanding of pivotal events in world history. They are written with a focus on providing readers with multiple perspectives to help them develop an appreciation for the complexity of the study of history. There is no set lens through which history must be viewed, and these titles encourage readers to analyze different viewpoints to understand why a historical figure acted the way they did or why a contemporary scholar wrote what they did about a historical event. In this way, readers are able to sharpen their critical-thinking skills and apply those skills in their history classes. Readers are aided in this pursuit by formally documented quotations and annotated bibliographies, which encourage further research and debate.

Many of these quotations come from carefully selected primary sources, including diaries, public records, and contemporary research and writings. These valuable primary sources help readers hear the voices of those who directly experienced historical events, as well as the voices of biographers and historians who provide a unique perspective on familiar topics. Their voices all help history come alive in a vibrant way.

As students read the titles in this series, they are provided with clear context in the form of maps, timelines, and informative text. These elements give them the basic facts they need to fully appreciate the high drama that is history.

The study of history is difficult at times—not because of all the information that needs to be memorized, but because of the challenging questions it asks us. How could something as horrible as the Holocaust happen? Why would religious leaders use torture during the Inquisition? Why does ISIS have so many followers? The information presented in each title gives readers the tools they need to confront these questions and participate in the debates they inspire.

As we pore over the stories of events and eras that changed the world, we come to understand a simple truth: No one can escape being a part of history. We are not bystanders; we are active participants in the stories that are being created now and will be written about in history books decades and even centuries from now. The titles in this series help readers gain a deeper appreciation for history and a stronger understanding of the connection between the stories of the past and the stories they are part of right now.

SETTING THE SCENE: A TIMELINE

1650 ·········· 1692–1693 ·········· 1824 ·········· 1848 ·········· 1850 ·········· 1872 ··········

Anne Bradstreet becomes the first American woman to have her poems published with her collection *The Tenth Muse Lately Sprung Up in America*.

The first public school for girls opens in Worcester, Massachusetts.

The first women's rights convention in the United States is held in Seneca Falls, New York, on July 19. Known as the Seneca Falls Convention, it is organized by Elizabeth Cady Stanton and Lucretia Mott.

Susan B. Anthony and 15 other women vote in the U.S. presidential election in Rochester, New York. All 16 women are arrested, and Anthony is put on trial and fined $100.

The first National Women's Rights Convention occurs October 23 and 24 in Worcester, Massachusetts. Lucy Stone is an organizer and participator in the event.

The Salem witch trials occur in Massachusetts Bay Colony, resulting in more than 200 arrested and 20 executed, most of them marginalized women of the community.

1888 ···· **1911** ···· **1917–1918** ···· **1920** ···· **1923** ···· **2017**

The International Council of Women (ICW) is formed. The ICW creates committees for women's rights and human rights issues such as suffrage, public health, and immigration.

Alice Paul leads the National Woman's Party in the "Silent Sentinels" protests outside of the White House.

The Equal Rights Amendment is introduced in the United States.

The 19th Amendment passes, giving American women the right to vote.

The Triangle Shirtwaist Factory fire in New York kills 146 people, mostly women. As a result of this, reform laws and fire prevention laws are passed to prevent a similar incident in the future.

On January 21, millions of women and men across the United States and around the world participate in protest marches to fight for their rights. The most publicized Women's March on Washington gathers 500,000 marchers.

"WOMEN'S RIGHTS ARE HUMAN RIGHTS"

Former U.S. first lady and presidential candidate Hillary Clinton once said, "Human rights are women's rights, and women's rights are human rights."[1] Achieving these rights has been a long, difficult struggle led by courageous women. For much of history, women were viewed as second-class citizens, and it was commonly believed that a woman's duty was staying at home, cooking, and raising a family. It was not until 1920 with the passage of the 19th Amendment to the U.S. Constitution that women even had the right to vote in the United States.

Women have worked incredibly hard to bring about change and progress from the status of second-class citizens with virtually no political or social rights to virtual equality with men under the law in many countries. This slow but steady march toward equality is often called the "women's movement." While important events in women's history have occurred worldwide and the fight for gender equality is not limited to America, the revolution that is called the "women's movement" has generally been centered in the United States. That term, along with formal writings about and studies of women's history and social progress, are all fairly recent phenomena. In fact, almost no books or essays existed to chronicle the struggles and achievements of women until the mid-1900s. Additionally, only when women began to receive educations comparable to men's did systematic studies of women's history start to emerge.

The State of Education

At first, little or no education for young women existed in places such as colonial America, except for what they learned from their parents in the home. Typically, a mother taught her daughter to cook, spin and weave, make clothes, and tend to other traditional "women's duties." In addition, a few girls were fortunate enough to have their parents

Hillary Clinton has spoken out about women's rights and ran for U.S. president in 2008 and 2016. Her presidential campaigns showcased both how far women have come and how much progress there is yet to make.

teach them reading and writing. Generally, however, literate women had few opportunities to use these skills, as society tended to frown on women expressing themselves in public, including in writing. In fact, in the 1800s, the Brontë sisters, who were famous British authors, all wrote under pen names to hide the fact that they were women—Charlotte Brontë wrote as Currer Bell, Emily wrote as Ellis Bell, and Anne wrote as Acton Bell. Elements of this inequity still existed even in the late 1990s, with *Harry Potter* author J. K. Rowling. Her publishers suggested she use the pen name of "J. K.," which was a combination of her full name of Joanne and her grandmother's name, Kathleen, because they believed young

boys would not want to read a book written by a woman.

Opportunities for learning finally began increasing, though at first very slowly, in the 1800s, and in 1837, Oberlin College in Ohio became the first institute of higher learning to admit both men and women in the United States.

Initially, however, the courses offered to women at such colleges were shorter and less complex than those offered to men. This was partly because the belief at the time was that women's brains were incapable of absorbing as much knowledge as men's. Also, the administrators and teachers at Oberlin and similar schools did not expect or desire their female graduates to go on to take the

Author J. K. Rowling was told to use a pen name because boys would not want to read the Harry Potter *series if it was written by a woman. The story and characters she created became some of the most loved in literature by readers young and old, male and female.*

kind of high-profile jobs traditionally performed by men.

Additionally, these institutions still discriminated against women by employing quota systems. As author Elizabeth K. Minnich explained,

> *Across higher education, quotas restricted women's access. Under Stanford [University]'s quota system, three males were accepted for every*

female. Histories of higher education reveal other uses of quotas. For many years there were quotas for Jews. Jewish women faced an at least double barrier, gender and religion, as did white ethnic working-class women who were not only limited by gender and poverty, but in some cases also by their Catholicism. Even when prestigious private men's universities opened their doors to women, admissions quotas were again set.[2]

Increasing Opportunities for Women

Fortunately, these quotas were removed as the 20th century progressed. However, women attending colleges and universities still could not study their own history in the courses offered in these schools. The historical narrative of women was ignored in both college curricula and virtually all history texts. To rectify what many people saw as an inexcusable situation, in the years that followed, scholars of both genders tackled the difficult task of writing accounts of women's historical experiences and struggles. One of the earliest successful examples was Abbie Graham's *Ladies in Revolt*, penned in 1934. However, studies of women's history really began to come of age in 1959, when three landmark books were published. One, Eleanor Flexner's *Century of Struggle: The Women's Rights Movement in the United States*, was the first comprehensive history of the 19th-century women's movement. In periodic updated versions, it remains one of the most important available books about women's history. The other two important works about women first released in 1959 were *A Century of Higher Education for American Women* by Mabel Newcomer and *Women and Work in America* by Robert Smuts. In addition, books such as Simone de Beauvoir's *The Second Sex* in 1949 and Betty Friedan's *The Feminine Mystique* in 1963 spoke of women's liberation and feminism. These important books became instant best sellers, and Friedan's book especially hinted toward change.

These milestones were followed by a flood of books about women's history, stimulated to a large degree by an upsurge of interest in social and family history that began in the 1960s. This soon led to the emergence of "women's studies" programs in colleges and universities. Before 1969, no such programs existed in the United States except for a few single courses on women's history. By the early 1990s, in contrast, more than 500 women's studies programs existed, most of which offered a major or minor degree.

Throughout the 20th century, the growing opportunities for women to become well educated and the increase of books and other resources examining women's history went hand-in-hand with the growth of feminism. Feminism is an organized, ongoing attempt by women to acquire social, political, and other rights equal to those of men. All of these aspects of women's lives—education, historical studies, and the fight for rights—have complemented and strengthened one another. Together, feminists around the world have worked and continue to work toward the day when all women are fully equal with men. In the words of University of Minnesota scholar Sara M. Evans, American women seek no special treatment, but rather only to "claim for themselves the status of full participants in the construction of the American dream."[3]

Angry Women Make Things Happen

Nearly 100 years after the passage of the 19th Amendment, which gave American women the right to vote, Hillary Clinton ran for U.S. president in 2008 and 2016, showing that a woman's duty was not just raising a family and that they can be powerful leaders. Clinton even won the popular vote in 2016, showing that much of the United States was ready for its first woman president. However, in the end, she lost the electoral vote to Donald Trump. Clinton's presidential run was even more remarkable considering the fact that at the time of her second campaign, American women had been allowed to vote for only 96 years.

Clinton's 2016 campaign was proof that while so much has been achieved throughout the women's movement, there is still much to be done. Even though Clinton was not the first

In 2017, thousands of people participated in women's marches around the world, with the largest event occurring in Washington, D.C. Participants created signs with empowering messages promoting equality and human rights.

woman to run for president, nor was it her first time running for president, a great deal of sexism came out during this time. For example, during one 2016 presidential election debate, Trump said Clinton was "such a nasty woman."[4]

The sexism that made itself known during this time, as well as the concern over health and reproductive rights, equality, gender-based violence, and more, was a catalyst for the historic Women's March on Washington on January 21, 2017, the day after Donald Trump's presidential inauguration. More than 500,000 women and men protested in Washington, D.C., and there were hundreds of marches across the United States and around the world. This protest promoted equality and human rights and showed the struggle that women continue to deal with every day. As the Women's March on Washington cofounder Tamika Mallory said,

We want to ensure that this country knows women are not happy … And when we get angry, change happens. We make things happen … This effort is not anti-Trump … This is pro-women. This is a continuation of a struggle women have been dealing with for a very long time. In this moment, we are connecting and being as loud as possible.[5]

CHAPTER ONE

SECOND-CLASS CITIZENS

While there is much to be done to achieve complete gender equality in present times, situations are much better for women in most cases than they were hundreds of years ago. Women were often considered second-class citizens in every way—politically, socially, and legally. Women were typically viewed as inferior to men, had no rights, and could not vote. Essentially, men had all the rights, and women, no matter what their social status was, had none. While upper-class women were in a better position than lower-class women, they still had no rights, especially to vote or run for a political office. However, while there were practices and laws in place to keep women in this position, women even in these early years rebelled against it.

Socially Acceptable Control

The attitude of the vast majority of men toward women hundreds of years ago was summed up by John Winthrop, leader of the Puritans in the 1630s and longtime governor of the Massachusetts Bay Colony. Feeling that men should maintain strict control over women, he said,

> He [the husband] is her [the wife's] lord, and she is to be subject to him, yet in a way of liberty, not of bondage; and a true wife accounts her subjection her honor and freedom, and would not think her condition safe and free, but in her subjection to her husband's authority … And if through forwardness and wantonness, etc., she shakes it [her husband's authority] off, at any time, she is at no rest in her spirit until she takes it up again.[6]

As a result of this superior male attitude, which was commonplace in that historical period, women had no legal rights to speak of. A married woman in late 17th-century America could not sign contracts. Nor could she keep and spend her own earnings (if she had a

John Winthrop, who governed Massachusetts Bay Colony, founded Boston under rigid religious and political policies that greatly oppressed women and placed them in the control of men.

job, which was rare), or sell property, even if she had inherited it. Moreover, a woman could not acquire custody of her children if she and her husband were legally separated. As for divorce, a woman could get one only in the most extreme circumstances—if her husband deserted her or brutally abused her on a regular basis. During these times, abuse caused outrage only if it was frequent and brutal, and a certain amount of abuse was considered socially acceptable. Men often used religion to rationalize this abuse and their authority over women. "The [American] colonists might be dissenters [someone who holds a different opinion] of one kind or another against the Church of England," the late, distinguished scholar Eleanor Flexner explained, "but they were at one with it in believing that woman's place was determined by limitations of mind and body, a punishment for the original sin of Eve."[7]

Women did not always submit to this authority, however. Some of them "used words to improve their reputations, to acquire a small degree of power in their communities, and even to express political opinions. They questioned males' ability to govern and used gossip to control stories about themselves and their neighbors. This type of disorderly speech was a threat to colonial officials."[8] In 1662, the General Assembly in Virginia passed a law that a riotous or quarrelsome wife could be plunged underwater as punishment for this type of gossip against her husband or neighbors.

Another notable aspect of early American women's second-class social status was that often they were not allowed to marry the man of their choice. This was partly because maintaining existing social ranks, or classes, was seen as imperative. As in most societies throughout history, a small group of well-to-do individuals made up society's upper class, while the bulk of the population was made up of people of limited means. The rich and powerful naturally desired to preserve the status quo, in which they dominated over the lower classes. Therefore, a woman marrying outside her social rank was frowned upon and even forbidden by many fathers.

Indentured Servitude

In addition to their plight as second-class citizens, colonial women endured lives filled with physically difficult and exhausting duties that they could not avoid. Married women were not the only females who faced this harsh reality. A large proportion of the women who came to North America in the 1600s were unmarried indentured servants. They were expected to work a set number of years for the man who paid their way across the ocean from England. According to historian David F. Hawke, a female indentured servant was legally bound

to serve out her indenture, and since the law forbade a servant to marry until she had completed her contract, that meant four or five years must pass before she could get a husband. They were devastating years. Exposure to malaria left her susceptible to more deadly diseases. The physical work was harder than anything she had known in England. If she served

DOCTRINE OF COVERTURE

During the settlement of Jamestown in the Virginia colony in the 1600s, the colonists were hoping to create the same social structure they had always known in England. This social structure consisted of a man having authority over his wife and every dependent member of his household, such as children. This social structure was further solidified by the doctrine of coverture. This doctrine affirmed that a woman was completely covered under her husband's person. In other words, he had complete control over her. A married woman had no legal status or rights and could not own property. Even if the wife brought the property to the marriage, once they were married, it became the husband's property. With this marriage, he also acquired all income and wages she earned.

An unmarried woman, however, could buy and sell properties, engage in contracts, and participate in other legal and business transactions. Some women with business skills were able to operate in society as though they were men. Anna Varlett Hack Boot, a Dutch settler, was able to carry on extensive trading activities while both single and married. Anne Toft, a single woman, was able to trade tobacco and fish with English and Dutch merchants. Toft was even able to acquire thousands of acres of land in Jamaica, Maryland, and Virginia in the 1660s. Toft and Boot are exceptional cases during this oppressive time. However, they were not the only women to engage in trading activities, buy and sell land, and protect their investments by going to court.

a small planter, she had, in addition to household chores, the fields to tend. She was easily exploited and degraded, for on an isolated farm there were few effective checks to the authority of the planter … If the woman lived through her service, a quick marriage was inevitable in a land where men outnumbered women seven to one.[9]

Even after single women did marry, their lives were still filled with hard, relentless work, including housework, yard work, and agricultural labor, and these duties were often done while a woman was pregnant and taking care of young children at the same time.

Accusations of Witchcraft

In addition to their many physical tasks and obligations, some early colonial women were also the targets of mean-spirited prejudices, superstitions, and suspicions of criminal acts because of a lingering belief in witches. The most famous example of such prejudice

The Salem witch trials have become closely associated with paranoia and injustice in colonial times as a result of more than 200 people being accused of witchcraft and 20 people being executed for it. The trials began because numerous girls in the village started having fits that including screaming and contortions.

took place in Salem, Massachusetts, in the 1690s. In 1692, 9-year-old Elizabeth Parris and 11-year old Abigail Williams started having fits that included screaming, contortions, and complaints of being pinched or bitten. Unable to come up with a medical reason for their fits, the local doctor, William Griggs, concluded the fits had supernatural causes and that the girls were bewitched. Samuel Parris, minister in the village and father of Elizabeth Parris, forced the girls to name the witch who was tormenting them. The girls started pointing fingers at members of the community, such as Tituba, a slave; Sarah Good, a beggar; and Sarah Osborne, an elderly woman. At the time, most people still believed that witches, sorcery, and demons were real. The result was one of the best documented cases of mass hysteria in history. Once the girls started pointing fingers and calling people witches, more girls started having fits. Whereas they originally said outcasts in the community were witches, once other girls started having fits, they started naming prominent members of the community—mostly women. In the end,

> more than 200 people were accused of practicing witchcraft—the Devil's magic—and 20 were executed. Eventually, the colony admitted the trials were a mistake and compensated the families of those convicted. Since then, the story of the trials has become synonymous with paranoia and injustice, and it continues to beguile *the popular imagination more than 300 years later.*[10]

Education to Improve One's Life

Opportunities for women to escape both their unrelenting physical labor and the prejudices against them were extremely limited. Over time, it became clear that education was the key, not only for men but also for women, to improving one's lot in life. The problem for women, however, was that at first, little or no educational opportunities existed for them, with occasional exceptions. The Puritans of Massachusetts Bay Colony, for instance, strongly emphasized learning and did allow some women to be taught reading and writing. One of them, Anne Bradstreet, enjoyed the distinction of being the first female American to become published in 1650. Part of one of her poems, titled "To My Dear and Loving Husband," reads,

> My love is such that rivers
>   cannot quench,
>
> Nor ought but love from thee
>   give recompense.
>
> Thy love is such I can no way repay;
>
> The heavens reward thee manifold,
>   I pray.

Anne Bradstreet, shown here, was the first American woman to have her written works published.

A PLEA FOR EQUALITY

In March 1776, Abigail Adams, wife of future U.S. president John Adams, wrote to him asking that, when he and his colleagues met to form a new nation, they would remember women's desire for greater rights and autonomy. Part of her letter stated,

> In the new code of laws which I suppose it will be necessary for you to make, I desire you would remember the ladies and be more generous and favorable to them than your ancestors.

> Do not put such unlimited power into the hands of the husbands.

> Remember, all men would be tyrants if they could. If particular care and attention is not paid to the ladies, we are determined to [stir up] a rebellion, and will not hold ourselves bound by any laws in which we have no voice or representation.

> That your sex are naturally tyrannical is a truth so thoroughly established as to admit of no dispute ...

> Regard us then as being placed by Providence [God or fate] under your protection, and ... make use of that power only for our happiness.[1]

1. Quoted in "Letters Between Abigail Adams and Her Husband John Adams," Liz Library, accessed January 6, 2018. www.thelizlibrary.org/suffrage/abigail.htm.

---

*Then while we live, in love let's
so [persevere]*

*That when we live no more, we may
live ever.*[11]

These words reveal that true love did exist between early colonial men and women. It is unclear, though, whether the poet's gratitude for being allowed to express herself in writing, a right possessed by few women at the time, accounted for some of her fond feelings for her husband. However, while Bradstreet was able to be published, most women in the 1600s, and even in the 1700s, could not read or write. They received no formal education, in part because most men felt they were not worthy of it. The famous 18th-century writer Jean-Jacques Rousseau stated the prevailing male attitude toward educating women. Rousseau believed, as did many men at the time, that women's duties were to support men:

> The whole education of women ought to be relative to men. To please them, to be useful to them, to make themselves loved and honored by them, to educate them when young, to care for them when grown, to counsel them, to console them, and to make life sweet and agreeable to them—these are the duties of women at all times, and what should be taught them from their infancy.[12]

Women during Rousseau's time did not have the social position to respond to him, and most could not read his words or write a response if they wanted to. Therefore, it was not until 1818 that a female Bostonian essayist, Hannah Mather Crocker, responded to Rousseau's position on women's education. In her book *Observations on the Real Rights of Women*, she stated, "There can be no doubt, but [that] there is as much difference in the powers of each individual of the male sex as there is of the female, and if [women] received the same mode of education, their [personal and social] improvement would be fully equal."[13]

The First U.S. Schools for Women

That Crocker was able to reach at least a small audience of readers in the early 1800s demonstrates that the idea of formal education for women was beginning to gain steam. A year after her book was published, New York governor DeWitt Clinton came out in support of an educational project proposed to him by Emma Willard, the wife of a Vermont physician. Willard wanted to establish a seminary, then meaning a private secondary school, for girls in their teens. The New York legislature approved the school's charter, and the town of Troy put up the money to build it. In 1821, the Troy Female Seminary became the first secondary, or preparatory, school (today called a high school) for young women in the United States. The students took courses in history, science, geography, and other subjects taught in secondary men's schools.

A downside to Willard's school was that it was private and required the girls to pay tuition (about $200 per year, then seen as a considerable sum). Most of the girls who attended it and other secondary schools that appeared in the years that followed came from wealthy families. Their parents were able to afford to hire tutors for them in their grade school, or elementary, years. Alternatively, the parents would teach them basic skills that prepared them for secondary school. Otherwise, the few secondary schools for girls that

Troy Female Seminary, shown here, was the first secondary school for girls in the United States.

existed at the time had no sources of new students. This was because before the 1820s, the country had only a tiny handful of free, or public, schools for children and none admitted girls. The first public school for girls opened in 1824 in Worcester, Massachusetts, and another appeared in New York City two years later.

Soon afterward, a movement to create public schools for girls gained momentum thanks to the efforts of a new generation of women writers who felt that women's social status should be equal to that of men. Among them was Scottish-born Frances Wright, often called Fanny Wright. Beginning in the late 1820s, she argued that women should achieve educations comparable to men's. That, she said, would be a crucial step in women's quest for social equality. Wright argued that women's equality was essential for a moral and advanced society. Wright delivered lectures on equality in New York City; Philadelphia, Pennsylvania; Boston,

Massachusetts; Baltimore, Maryland; and other U.S. cities in the 1830s and 1840s. Many of those who attended were women, but quite often, she spoke to audiences of men as well. Some men viewed her as a dangerous radical out to ruin traditional society. Others, however, thought that her arguments made good sense, and as a result, her social influence grew over the years. The right of women to receive a decent education, along with the larger cause of women's social equality, advanced significantly, thanks to her tireless efforts. These accomplishments inspired a later activist for women's rights, Ernestine L. Rose, to declare in 1858:

> *Frances Wright was the first woman in this country who spoke on the equality of the sexes. She had indeed a hard task before her. The elements [existing social attitudes] were entirely unprepared. She had to break up the time-hardened soil of conservatism [traditional values and beliefs], and her reward was sure—the same reward that is always bestowed upon those who are in the vanguard of any great movement. She was subjected to public odium [hatred], slander, and persecution. But these were not the only things she received. Oh, she had her reward!—that reward of which no enemies could deprive her, which no slanders could make less precious— the eternal reward of knowing that she had done her duty.*[14]

Shattering the First Barrier to Equality

Even as the barriers against elementary and secondary schools for young women were breaking, women's rights activists were working to establish schools of higher learning for women.

Oberlin College, which was founded in Ohio in 1833, began admitting women a few years later. The first female to take a full schedule of courses there graduated in 1841. Soon afterward, Oberlin awarded a degree to Lucy Stone, who went on to become one of the nation's leading abolitionists, suffragists, and vocal advocates for women's rights. One of her fellow graduates, Antoinette Brown, became the first woman in the United States to be ordained a minister.

In this same period, an educator and women's rights activist named Catharine Beecher appeared on the scene. As a young woman in the late 1820s, she had run a small secondary school for girls in Connecticut. In time, Beecher became increasingly concerned that young women get good educations. In the 1830s, tens of thousands of young men from the East, searching for adventure or better lives, headed for the Midwest and West. Those who were married took their wives with them or sent for them later. However, many of these men were unmarried, which drained the existing pool of prospective husbands for single women in the East, leaving large numbers of young women unmarried and needing to support themselves.

A large proportion of these women took jobs in factories in eastern manufacturing towns such as Lowell, Massachusetts. By the early 1850s, Lowell had the largest manufacturing complex in the country and employed many thousands of women, most of them single. In such factories in eastern towns, women worked long hours for little pay and often endured unsanitary or dangerous working conditions, or a combination of both.

It would be better, Beecher said, if more women who needed jobs became teachers. In her view, one shared by growing numbers of women and even a few men, teaching was a safer, more dignified profession. (She also promoted the idea of women becoming nurses and childcare professionals.) As a result, Beecher developed a plan for building a chain of "normal schools," or colleges to train teachers, in the Midwest. One of the schools she helped to make a reality—Milwaukee-Downer College for women in Wisconsin—was in operation until 1964, when it merged with Lawrence University. To rally support for her plan, in 1852, Beecher founded the American Women's Educational Association. Later generations came

Oberlin College, shown here, began admitting women in the 1830s. Lucy Stone, an influential abolitionist and suffragist, graduated from Oberlin.

to see her as one of the "founding mothers" of modern teachers' training.

Emma Willard also played a role in demanding the proper training of teachers. Due to the status of their own education, women who became teachers had no training. Additionally, since they had no training, they could not receive the same salaries as male teachers, who often had college degrees, did. To address this issue, Willard started the Willard Association for the Mutual Improvement of Female Teachers in 1837. This was the first organization to bring attention to the matter of teacher training and salaries.

Besides providing thousands of women with paying jobs, another outcome of Willard and Beecher's work was that teaching became a respected profession dominated by women. For the first time, large numbers of American women could work outside the home in a job that required an education comparable to that of the average educated man. Also, teaching was a profession in which women principally used their minds and personal talents, as opposed to breaking their backs and spirits doing unrelenting physical labor.

In this way, the first major barrier to female social equality in the United States was shattered. Many successful female teachers, nurses, and other professional women of

that era affectionately remembered a passage from one of Frances Wright's more popular lectures: "However novel it may appear," she declared, "I shall venture the assertion that, until women assume the place in society which good sense and good feeling alike assign to them, human improvement must advance but feebly."[15]

CHAPTER TWO

LAUNCHING THE MOVEMENT

The fight for, and eventual granting of, educational opportunities was a major victory in the women's movement. With this victory, the fight for women's rights increasingly gained attention and was especially boosted during the period of the American Civil War, from 1861 to 1865. The abolitionist movement led to the growth of the women's movement, with which it shared many supporters. These people truly believed in equality for all and fought for abolition with the same fervor that they fought for women's rights. Many of these people saw a natural parallel between racial equality and gender equality and felt justified in supporting the fight for women's rights along with the battle to end slavery. According to Eleanor Flexner and Ellen Fitzpatrick,

Thousands of men and women were drawn into the [antislavery] work; among the latter were the first conscious feminists, who would go to school in the struggle to free the slaves and, in the process, launch their own fight for equality. It was in the abolition movement that women first learned to organize, to hold public meetings, to conduct petition campaigns. As abolitionists they first won the right to speak in public, and began to evolve a philosophy of their place in society and of their basic rights. For a quarter of a century the two movements, to free the slave and liberate the woman, nourished and strengthened one another.[16]

Fighting to End Slavery

The abolitionist movement, which captured the hearts and minds of thousands of American women and taught them how to organize a movement, first began in England and France in the late 1700s. As it gained momentum, it spread across the Atlantic to the recently established United States.

At first, the abolitionists aimed their attacks on the Atlantic slave trade. In a growing torrent of books, newspaper articles, and public speeches, they condemned the buying and selling of human beings. Abolitionists also convinced many religious leaders to join the cause, which gave the movement more weight in the minds of many people. The result of these efforts was impressive. In 1807, Britain banned the slave trade and the importation of Africans into its territories worldwide. The United States followed suit in the following year.

However, these victories over injustice marked only the beginning of the abolitionist movement. In the decades that followed, it began to target the slavery institution itself and set the daunting goal of wiping it out for good. Although some American men became abolitionists, considerable numbers of American women were drawn to the cause. Because women were treated as social inferiors themselves, many of them sympathized with the plight of black slaves. Additionally, female abolitionists recognized early on that winning the fight against slavery could also earn them increased respect and make them a social and political force to be reckoned with. As scholar Shirley J. Yee wrote, "The fact that abolitionists were already wrestling with the issue of racial equality as a goal of the movement created a climate ripe for discussions of equality between the sexes."[17]

The result was that at first hundreds and later many thousands of women threw themselves into antislavery activities. They included both whites and free blacks living in the North. One prominent black abolitionist was Philadelphia's Grace Bustill Douglass, who helped to establish the Philadelphia Female Anti-Slavery Society in 1833. Her daughter Sarah Douglass spent more than 40 years fighting for educational opportunities for African American children, both male and female. Another noted black female abolitionist, Harriet Tubman, was born a slave and eventually escaped from a Maryland plantation. She courageously returned to the South several times to help free hundreds of slaves and lead them to safety in the North.

One of the more prominent white female abolitionists was Lucretia Coffin Mott. She and her husband, James, were among the leaders of the Free Produce Movement, which employed the tactic of boycotting goods produced by Southern slaves, especially cotton. Two other white antislavery activists, sisters Sarah and Angelina Grimké of South Carolina, tirelessly traveled through the North giving speeches denouncing slavery. They also consistently linked the issues of slaves' freedom and women's equality. Some men in the movement asked them to stop talking about women's rights because they felt it diluted the antislavery message. However, they refused to stop: "If we surrender the right to speak in public

Harriet Tubman escaped from slavery and then helped hundreds of slaves escape by leading them to the North.

135,000 SETS, 270,000 VOLUMES SOLD.

UNCLE TOM'S CABIN

FOR SALE HERE.

AN EDITION FOR THE MILLION, COMPLETE IN 1 Vol., PRICE 37 1-2 CENTS.
"   "   IN GERMAN, IN 1 Vol., PRICE 50 CENTS.
"   "   IN 2 Vols,. CLOTH, 6 PLATES, PRICE $1.50.
SUPERB ILLUSTRATED EDITION, IN 1 Vol., WITH 153 ENGRAVINGS,
PRICES FROM $2.50 TO $5.00.

The Greatest Book of the Age.

Harriet Beecher Stowe persuaded many people to support the abolition of slavery through her book Uncle Tom's Cabin. Uncle Tom's Cabin *became a best seller that is still considered a classic today.*

this year," Angelina told the men, "we must surrender the right to petition next year, and the right to write the year after, and so on. What then can women do for the slave, when she herself is under the feet of man and shamed into silence?"[18]

Although thousands of other women played important roles in the abolitionist movement, none had a bigger ultimate impact against slavery than Harriet Beecher Stowe. The daughter of a Northern minister, in 1852, she published *Uncle Tom's Cabin*. It was the fictional story of a virtuous Christian slave named Tom who is viciously beaten to death by his brutal master. Stowe's book became an enormous best seller and persuaded large numbers of Americans to support the abolition of slavery. When President Abraham Lincoln met Stowe during the Civil War, he said, "So you are the little woman who wrote the book that made this great war."[19]

Overall, the contribution that female lecturers, writers, and other activists made to the antislavery movement was central to its eventual success. The famous African American writer and abolitionist Frederick Douglass paid tribute to that contribution. "When the true history of the anti-slavery cause shall be written," he said, "women will occupy a large space in its pages, for the cause of the slave has been peculiarly women's cause. Her heart and her conscience have supplied in large degree its motive and mainspring."[20]

Seneca Falls, New York

Some of the courageous and hardworking women Douglass had spoken so highly of felt that they could not wait until slavery was eliminated to begin organizing a movement for their own rights. Lucretia Mott and Elizabeth Cady Stanton decided to act on that feeling.

Mott and Stanton had first met at the World Anti-Slavery Convention in London, England, in 1840. Caught up in the excitement of that huge gathering of educated, passionate people, they discussed the idea of organizing a similar meeting for the advancement of women. However, several years passed before they were both in a position to transform their idea into reality.

In the early summer of 1848, Mott, Stanton, and three other women, Jane Hunt, Martha Wright, and Mary Ann McClintock, met in Waterloo, New York, near Seneca Falls. They committed themselves to launching a movement for women's rights. Then, they drafted an announcement to advertise an event, which appeared in the July 14 issue of the *Seneca County Courier* and read,

Women's Rights Convention—A convention to discuss the social, civil, and religious rights of women will be held in the Wesleyan Chapel, Seneca Falls, New York, on Wednesday and Thursday, the 19th and 20th of July current; commencing at 10 a.m. During the first day the meeting will

be held exclusively for women, who are earnestly invited to attend. The public generally are invited to be present on the second day, when Lucretia Mott of Philadelphia and other ladies and gentlemen will address the convention.[21]

To the organizers' surprise, despite the stipulation that women only should attend on the first day, 40 men, including Frederick Douglass, showed up. Around 240 women also arrived, after which a long series of discussions and speeches ensued. One of the most emotional and memorable was given by Stanton. She said, in part,

The time [has] fully come for the question of woman's wrongs to be laid before the public. [I believe] that woman herself must do this work—for woman alone can understand the height and the depth, the length and the breadth of her degradation and woe. Man cannot speak for us—because he has been educated to believe that we differ from him so materially, that he cannot judge of our thoughts, feelings and opinions by his own …

Among the many important questions which have been brought before the public, there is none that more vitally affects the whole human family than that which is technically termed Woman's rights. Every allusion to the degraded and inferior position occupied by woman all over the world, has

ever been met by scorn and abuse. [We here today] dare assert that woman stands by the side of man—his equal, placed here by her God to enjoy with him the beautiful earth, which is her home as it is his—having the same sense of right and wrong and looking to the same Being for guidance and support.[22]

"Declaration of Sentiments and Resolutions"

A few days before Stanton made her groundbreaking speech at the convention, she had drafted an important document. Called the "Declaration of Sentiments and Resolutions," it is in the style and format of the U.S. Declaration of Independence. All who attended the gathering endorsed the ideas contained in this document. The beginning of Stanton's declaration stated,

When, in the course of human events, it becomes necessary for one portion of the family of man to assume among the people of the earth a position different from that which they have hitherto occupied, but one to which the laws of nature and of nature's God entitle them, a decent respect to the opinions of mankind requires that they should declare the causes that impel them to such a course.

We hold these truths to be self-evident: that all men and women are created

Just as ridicule today often has a squelching [stifling] effect on new ideas, this attack in the press caused many people from the Convention to rethink their positions. Many of the women who had attended the convention were so embarrassed by the publicity that they actually withdrew their signatures from the Declaration. But most stood firm. And something the editors had not anticipated happened. Their negative articles about the women's call for expanded rights were so livid and widespread that they actually had a positive impact far beyond anything the organizers could have hoped for. People in cities and isolated towns alike were now alerted to the issues, and joined this heated discussion of women's rights in great numbers ...

The Seneca Falls women had optimistically hoped for "a series of conventions embracing every part of the country." And that's just what did happen.[26]

In fact, so many regional gatherings of women took place that a national women's convention became inevitable. The first National Women's Rights Convention occurred in 1850 in Worcester, Massachusetts. While several people organized the convention, Lucy Stone and Pauline Wright Davis were the primary organizers. Lucy Stone, who had both money and connections in high places, presided as president at the convention. Her involvement in the movement helped it grow and attract a number of new, socially prominent members. Among them were America's first female ordained minister, Antoinette Brown; noted lecturer Elizabeth Oakes Smith; and the dynamic African American writer and lecturer Sojourner Truth.

Between 1850 and 1860, national women's rights conventions were held in every year except 1857. In 1852, the convention returned to its Upstate New York roots by holding the third National Women's Rights Convention in Syracuse, New York. Lucretia Mott presided over the convention. She silenced one minister who offended many participants by speaking on the biblical basis of women's rights.

Meanwhile, smaller regional and local gatherings took place in most of the states in the North. During these years, the press remained mostly hostile to women's efforts to achieve equal rights. "What do the leaders of the women's rights convention want?" one editor asked. Answering his own question, he went on, "They want to vote and ... be members of Congress, and in the heat of debate subject themselves to coarse jests and indecent language."[27] Other newspaper editorials were even more critical and scornful and stated that women should not be allowed to step out of what were considered their normal duties in life.

Abraham Lincoln was the most powerful American to express his feelings about women's help during the Civil War.

The Civil War

The women who attended the conventions and otherwise promoted women's rights reached a sort of crossroads at the outbreak of the Civil War in 1861. Some wanted to press on with their struggle for equality. However, many others felt that they should put such efforts on hold during the conflict, an enormous event that to one degree or another affected the lives of nearly all Americans. The majority of women, therefore, white, black, Southerner, and Northerner alike, had two main goals during the hostilities. These were to ensure that they and their families survived and to aid in the war effort. While many women provided first-aid care to do their part in the war effort, some women took it a step further. Historians have documented at least 240 cases of women, both Northerners and Southerners, disguising themselves as men and fighting alongside male soldiers. Larger numbers of women chose to help the troops by taking over a wide range of jobs. Many ran family farms or businesses while their husbands were away fighting. Others served as clerks in government offices, as postal workers, and as seamstresses sewing soldiers' uniforms.

At the end of the war in 1865, American women once more found themselves at a crossroads. The organized fight for their rights had been resting on the back burner during the battle between North and South. However, the work they had done during the war was so impressive that they had greatly enhanced their image in the eyes of men, including those in power. The most powerful of all, President Lincoln, remarked: "If all that has been said by orators and poets since the creation of the world were applied to the women of America, it would not do them justice for their conduct during this war."[28]

Thus, women facing the postwar years were more enthusiastic than ever about their chances for enhancing their social status. According to historian Harriet Sigerman, at the war's end, women's rights activists "forged ahead, ready to labor for their freedom. From their battles emerged many new ideas for achieving social and political equality for women."[29]

CHAPTER THREE

FIGHTING FOR THE RIGHT TO VOTE

Even though women helped immensely during the Civil War and prominent people such as Abraham Lincoln praised their efforts, after the war, they were still not seen as men's equals. They were a bit more respected, but many people did not even slightly consider granting women the right to vote. Additionally, women were not paid the same amount as men for the same amount of work—a battle that still continues in 2018. In February 1869, a letter was sent to the *New York Times* questioning why female and male government employees were not paid the same. At that time, there were 500 women employed by the Treasury Department of the U.S. government, and they made half as much as men who were employed by the same department. The author of the article stated, "Very few persons deny the justice of the principle that equal work should command equal pay without regard to the sex of the laborer ... But it is one thing to acknowledge the right of a principle and quite another to practice it."[30] While the constant lack of equality was immensely frustrating, by no means did it stop or slow down the movement.

Race and Equality

Another dimension of the struggle for equal pay and voting rights involved race and the differing realities of life for white and black women. If the road toward voting rights and equality seemed long for white women, it appeared even longer for African American women. Thanks to the war, all black women were now free. However, the fact that they had long been enslaved and that they were African American put them in a more difficult position than that of white women. Most white Americans still viewed blacks as less intelligent than, as well as morally inferior to, themselves.

That meant things were even harder for African American women. For the most part, the only work open to them was the same as when they were enslaved. Also, they received the lowest wages of any segment of the population. This wage gap has continued even in the 2000s. According to a 2016 study by the Pew Research Center, black women make 65 cents for every dollar a white man makes, whereas Hispanic women make 58 cents for every dollar a white man makes.

In the immediate postwar years, therefore, most black women, especially in the South, did not see it a realistic option to spend time demanding the right to vote and fighting for women's rights. They focused instead on seeing that their families survived and that their children had at least a chance for a better life in the future. According to Flexner and Fitzpatrick,

Few freedwomen could indulge in full-time homemaking, because their families needed their economic contribution. Most black women did the same work in freedom that they had done in bondage—they worked in the fields or as mid-wives or domestic servants. Or they peddled poultry, eggs, fruit, and vegetables along the roads or at markets. But with freedom, something was different. To their way of thinking, they worked for their families, not for their employers, and these women organized their working life around family

needs. Their sense of well-being was closely linked to their families' well-being. One mother, a cook, claimed that she could die happy, though she had spent much of her life in bondage, because her children would grow up in freedom.[31]

Exclusion of Women's Voting Rights

Meanwhile, those women, white and black, who possessed the time and means to continue the struggle for women's rights came up against some unexpected obstacles. They had anticipated that after the war Congress would amend the Constitution to reflect the fact that slavery had been abolished. In their view, this presented a great opportunity to deal with women's lack of suffrage, or the right to vote. Hopefully lawmakers would word the new law so as to give both blacks and women that basic right.

However, many women were disappointed when the 14th Amendment did not address their chief grievance. Ratified in 1868, the amendment defined citizenship for African Americans. Moreover, to the discontent of Stanton and other activists, it used the word "male" three times, which they felt seemed to question whether women were citizens at all. Stanton complained that the amendment created "an antagonism between black men and all women" that

Fortieth Congress of the United States of America;

At the *third* Session.

Begun and held at the city of Washington, on Monday, the *seventh* day of *December*, one thousand eight hundred and *sixty-eight*.

A RESOLUTION

Proposing an amendment to the Constitution of the United States.

Resolved by the Senate and House of Representatives of the United States of America in Congress assembled, (two-thirds of both Houses concurring) That the following article be proposed to the legislatures of the several States as an amendment to the Constitution of the United States, which, when ratified by three-fourths of said legislatures shall be valid as part of the Constitution, namely:

Article XV.

Section 1. The right of citizens of the United States to vote shall not be denied or abridged by the United States or by any State on account of race, color, or previous condition of servitude —

Section 2. The Congress shall have power to enforce this article by appropriate legislation —

Schuyler Colfax
Speaker of the House of Representatives.

B. F. Wade
President of the Senate pro tempore.

Attest:
Ed. McPherson
Clerk of House of Representatives.

Geo. C. Gorham
Secy of Senate U.S.

The 15th Amendment, the text of which is shown here, granted all citizens the right to vote but also asserted that it was only men who had that right, not women.

would allow men to continue dominating women, "especially in the southern states."[32]

Stanton and her colleagues were no less dissatisfied with the 15th Amendment, ratified in 1870. It guaranteed the right to vote to all citizens regardless of race and asserted that men had the right to vote. Previously, only state laws regulated voting rights—it was the first time the Constitution had made a decision on the same issue. Elizabeth Cady Stanton wrote, "If that word 'male' be inserted, it will take us a century at least to get it out."[33] The activists questioned why the lawmakers had not included "sex" or "gender" along with race and color, which would have given women the vote. Various men in high positions were quick to answer these questions. One, a senator from Oregon, declared,

The woman who undertakes to put her sex in an adversary position to man, who undertakes by the use of some independent political power [that is, voting] to contend and fight against man, displays a spirit which would, if able, convert all the now harmonious elements of society into a state of war.[34]

Not surprisingly, the leaders of the women's movement were furious at such attempts to demean women and rationalize denying them suffrage. Stanton lashed out at such male attacks and the 15th Amendment itself, saying,

There is no true patriotism, no true nobility in tamely and silently submitting to this insult. [It] is licking the hand that forges a new chain for our degradation. It is endorsing the old idea that woman's divinely ordained position is at man's feet, and not on an even platform by his side, [so that] the women of the Republic are now [expected] to touch the lowest depths of their political degradation.[35]

At this point, it was clear to women's rights activists that their struggle to win suffrage was going to be long and difficult. The question was how they should go about achieving this goal. Some of them, including Stanton and Susan B. Anthony, condemned the 15th Amendment. Anthony, meanwhile, took the right to vote into her own hands by voting with 15 other women in Rochester, New York. The women registered and voted in the national presidential election and were subsequently arrested. Anthony was the only one to be put on trial, and hers was a test case of sorts—she would be found not guilty if she was able to convince the jury that she had a right under the U.S. Constitution to vote. Therefore, all women in the United States would have the right to vote. However, Anthony was found guilty and fined $100.

Stanton was furious that women had not gained the vote along with black men. Other self-identified moderates of the group felt the better course was to endorse the 15th Amendment and remain inclusive of all groups in the ongoing fight for women's rights. They decided to break away from those they labeled extremists. Largely under the leadership of activist Lucy Stone, in 1869, the moderates formed the American Woman Suffrage Association. That same year, Stanton and Anthony established a rival organization, the National Woman Suffrage Association, with Stanton as director. Although the members of these groups did not then foresee the consequences, this split in the women's movement proved counterproductive. It watered down its energies and impact and likely caused the struggle for female voting rights to go on longer than it would have if the activists had remained united.

International Women's Organizations

In 1882 and 1883, Stanton and Anthony traveled to England and France to meet with women's rights reformers and attempt to start an international suffrage organization. The effort did not materialize until 1888 when the National Woman Suffrage Association invited international representatives to their conference in Washington, D.C. The International Council of Women (ICW) was created from this meeting. The idea was for existing women's rights groups to organize into national councils, then they would join the ICW. The first council was formed in the United States, followed by countries including Canada, Sweden, Denmark, the Netherlands, Germany, Australia, and Great Britain. By 1914, there were 23 national councils, and by 1939, there were 36.

In 1899, the ICW formed committees committed to the legal position of married women and peace, and it later added committees for suffrage, immigration, public health, and more. As of 2018, the ICW still fights for the advancement of women around the world and has played a role in important events. The ICW had a hand in the formation of the United Nations (UN) Charter when the UN was created to ensure that women's equal rights were included. According to the ICW, the organization

empowers women through a range of projects and programs designed to help women to help themselves in practical actions including:

- *Equal rights and responsibilities for women and men*

- *Peace and understanding through international co-operation, negotiation and reconciliation*

- *The fuller integration of women as decision-makers in peace-making and peace building efforts*

- *Human rights for all people*

- *The elimination of all forms of discrimination*

- *Sustainable development*

- *Communication and networking worldwide*[36]

However, like the division between Lucy Stone's and Stanton's groups, there were also members of the ICW who did not agree with some positions the organization took. As a response to this, Lida Gustava Heymann and Anita Augspurg helped form the International Alliance of Women. The alliance had a goal of meeting every two years in a different country to stimulate suffrage activity. The first national groups were in Australia, Germany, the Netherlands, the United States, Sweden, and Great Britain. By 1913, this number had grown to 26, and by 1929, it had grown to 51.

Originally, the alliance focused only on suffrage. However, around the time of World War I and when women finally received the right to vote in the United States, the alliance began focusing on other issues, including equal pay, and still focused on suffrage in places where women had not yet received the right to vote.

Once again, a new organization formed out of the International Alliance of Women. This organization had a focus of peace during a time when war was breaking out. The Women's International League for Peace and Freedom formed when the alliance had halted their meetings because of World War I. In 1915, in The Hague, a group of

women from both the neutral and warring countries, including Austria, Belgium, Britain, Canada, Denmark, Germany, Hungary, Italy, the Netherlands, Norway, Sweden, and the United States, met and called for continuous mediation, women's enfranchisement, the establishment of an international society of nations, the convening of a congress of women alongside the peace conference that would follow the war, and ... the sending of envoys from the congress to the belligerent and neutral nations in an attempt to end the war.[37]

The group had 13 national sections in 1915, which grew to 22 in 1921. The group stuck to their goals they set up in 1915, which were emancipation of women and peace.

These international groups were incredibly important to issues worldwide. Women from many different countries came together for common causes and to better the situation of women in other areas. As the Institute of European History published on its European History Online website,

The women of the Council, Alliance and League shared not only a desire to gather across national borders but also an interest in their status as women in both national and global arenas. They perceived their femaleness as part of what defined the boundaries of their group, but their feminist consciousness went beyond any simple commonality of biology or socialization. Although they disagreed about precisely how to do so, they sought to improve their situation as women. Some claimed the label "feminist," others avoided it. There wasn't complete agreement about any one aspect of the feminist program either. They did, however, share a sense of themselves as a group with interests distinct from those of men; a perception that existing societal arrangements, differing as they did from country to country, disadvantaged women in relation to men; and a commitment to improving women's place in society.[38]

Substandard Workplace Conditions

The equal pay rights that these international groups were fighting for was a fight that had been going on for decades. In the first few decades of the 19th century, the Industrial Revolution, which had begun in Britain in the previous century, began to take hold in the United States. Numerous factories were built, mostly in the northern states. At first, most of these factories manufactured various kinds of textiles, and they primarily hired women.

One major reason that the owners of these businesses hired so many women was that, by long-standing custom, women made far less than men did in the same jobs. (For instance, in the early 1830s, female printers in most northern cities made about 50 cents a day, whereas their male counterparts made three times that amount.) Hiring women therefore allowed factory owners to make higher profits.

Besides paying women low wages, these owners took advantage of them in other ways. For example, most female workers had few or no chances for advancement. Also, they often had to pay fines for making mistakes and endured unhealthy or dangerous working conditions, or sometimes a combination of both. These included workweeks between 60 and 80 hours long, inadequate lighting, poor ventilation, clothes or limbs getting caught in machines, fires, and building collapses.

As time went on, some courageous women stepped forward to try to reform the substandard conditions of their workplaces. One approach was to demand equal pay, or at least more than the poor wages most women received. However, at a time when women still could not vote and had no say in politics or making laws, the concept of equal pay, or comparable worth, was viewed as extremely radical. Therefore, requests for higher wages generally fell on deaf ears. Strides toward equal pay were not made until the 20th century. However, even in the 21st century, there is still a large gap between men's and women's wages. According to a 2016

AVERAGE DAILY WAGES OF MEN AND WOMEN IN 1885

	adult males (dollars)	adult females	
		dollars	percent of adult-male wages
boots and shoes	2.05	1.24	60
boxes	2.26	0.65	29
carpetings	1.51	1.19	79
carriages and wagons	2.00	1.15	58
clocks and watches	2.00	1.60	80
clothing	1.72	0.91	53
cotton goods	1.26	0.87	69
glass	2.98	1.85	62
jute goods	1.55	0.85	55
leather	1.92	1.35	70
musical instruments	2.10	1.50	72
paper	1.64	0.96	59
print works	1.66	0.91	55
rubber	1.70	1.10	65
silk	2.27	1.31	58
tobacco	1.33	0.85	64
woolen goods	1.49	1.00	67
miscellaneous	1.96	0.81	41

According to this information from the National Bureau of Economic Research, depending on the industry, American women made between 29 percent and 80 percent of what a man would make for the same job in 1885.

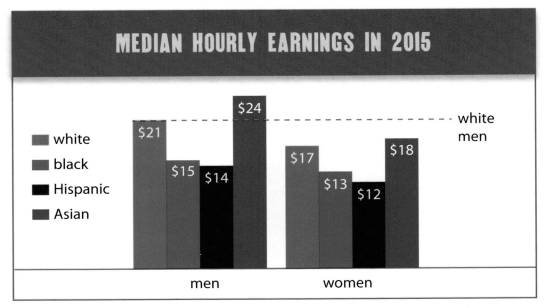

MEDIAN HOURLY EARNINGS IN 2015

white men

- white
- black
- Hispanic
- Asian

men: $21, $15, $14, $24

women: $17, $13, $12, $18

According to this information from the Pew Research Center, white men earned higher hourly wages than everyone except Asian men in the United States in 2015.

study by the Pew Research Center, white women make 82 cents for every dollar a man makes. According to this same study, 27 percent of women said that being a woman made it harder for them to succeed, whereas 7 percent of men said their gender made it harder for them to succeed. Additionally, 30 percent of the men in the study stated that their gender made it easier for them to succeed, whereas 8 percent of women said their gender made it easier for them to succeed.

Reform Through Strikes

Another approach to reform, one tried frequently by American women workers, was going on strike. The first known strike of American female mill workers on their own (as opposed to women striking along with men) took place in Dover, New Hampshire, in 1828. Several hundred women astonished the community by walking out of the mill and staging a loud demonstration. They were protesting unfair new factory rules, including not allowing any talking on the job and imposing monetary fines on those late for work. Unfortunately for the women, nothing was gained. The owners made no concessions, fired the strike's organizers, and intimidated the others into returning to work by threatening to replace them with "better behaved women."[39]

The New Hampshire incident also set a precedent. Of the dozens of strikes launched by female workers in the 19th century, few achieved even moderate success. Not until a 1909 walkout of shirtwaist (a women's blouse tailored to look like a shirt) makers in New York City did American factory women win a major victory against their employers.

A somewhat more effective approach in the slow but steady movement to reform women's working conditions was the formation of unions. In the late 1800s and early 1900s, women's unions had little or no political influence. However, they could help women help themselves through a variety of activities. For example, the Women's Trade Union League (WTUL) was established in 1903 by combining several smaller unions that represented female factory workers. The WTUL provided money, publicity, and other aid to smaller women's unions; supported individual strikes by women in industry in numerous cities; found meeting rooms where women could discuss their workplace grievances; helped women report labor law violations to the authorities; paid doctors to examine workers with health problems; and investigated working conditions in factories. After such investigations, the union informed the public about the substandard working conditions it had found. A pamphlet the WTUL published about adverse conditions in many textile mills said in part: "The weavers, the ring-spinners, the speeder-tenders, work in heat which is like the intense heat of the tropics, and at the end of the day's work [they] face the bitter cold nights of our northern winters. What a price we are paying for our cotton sheets and our calico."[40]

As time went on, the WTUL became even better organized and more effective. In 1907, its leaders adopted more challenging goals designed to aid working women, including securing "for girls and women equal opportunity with boys and men in trades and technical training and pay on the basis of occupation and not on the basis of sex."[41] Also, in 1909, the union started lobbying legislators for an eight-hour workday and minimum wages for women. As a result, 14 states adopted such wage laws between 1913 and 1923.

Reform Through Disasters

Despite the hard work and dedication of thousands of members of the women's labor movement, a considerable portion of workplace reforms were driven by public outrage over industrial disasters. The most notable example was the 1911 Triangle Shirtwaist Factory fire.

Owned by Max Blanck and Isaac Harris, the company had a history of corruption. The owners had a history of suspicious fires—the Triangle factory burned in 1902, and the Diamond Waist factory burned in both 1907 and 1910.

The Triangle Shirtwaist Factory fire, shown here, inspired safety laws. The tragedy caused 146 people to die in the fire or by jumping from the building, which did not have a sprinkler system to help put out the fire.

REMEMBERING THE TRIANGLE FIRE

Since the 1970s, commemorative events have been held on the anniversary of the Triangle Shirtwaist Factory fire. Hundreds attend, and descendants of victims read passages. Workers who are still fighting for their rights share remarks. In addition, the names of the victims are read aloud, and the same fire department ladder company that responded to the fire in 1911 raises a ladder to the seventh floor, which was the highest floor the ladder could reach in 1911. Cara Noel, of the American Federation of Labor and Congress of Industrial Organizations (AFL-CIO) stated that the commemorative events are "a way of showing that workers have common struggles, and that there is a need for us to continue to stand together as a movement." Noel added that the purpose of the events are "to remember the past, to help in the present and to set the pace for the future ... It is also important to recognize the current worker fights in New York City including immigration justice, raising wages, the right to organize, income inequality and safe workplaces."[1]

Since the 1970s, hundreds of people, including the descendants of victims, have held a ceremony at the location of the Triangle Shirtwaist Factory fire. They hold up shirts with a victim's name and age on each one to remember them.

1. Quoted in Rosemary Feitelberg, "Five Hundred Supporters Expected at 106th Anniversary of the Triangle Shirtwaist Factory Fire," WWD, March 23, 2017. wwd.com/fashion-news /fashion-scoops/five-hundred-supporters-106th-anniversary-of-the-triangle-shirtwaist-factory-fire-10850476/.

Union workers marched in demonstrations to honor the victims of the Triangle Shirtwaist Factory fire.

Historians theorize the owners deliberately set the buildings on fire to collect on insurance policies. While this is not the direct cause of the Triangle Shirtwaist Factory fire, it contributed to it because the owners refused to install sprinkler systems. In addition, out of four elevators, only one was operational. There were two stairways that led to the street, but one door only opened inward and the other was always locked from the outside to prevent theft. Additionally, the fire escape was incredibly narrow—it would have taken hours for all the workers to use it.

More than 400 women labored in the company's 10-story building near Washington Square in New York City. On March 25, a fire started on the eighth floor in a rag bin. The manager attempted to use a hose to put out the fire, but as with other things in the factory, the hose was not in good condition—it was rotted and the valve was rusted shut. The operational elevator could hold only 12 people, and it made only 4 trips before it broke down. Others were not so lucky. Some tried to escape via the stairs but encountered a locked door and were trapped. Others leaped from windows and fell to their deaths. Many fell on the fire hoses, which made it difficult to begin putting out the fire. A total of 146 workers, almost all women, perished in the disaster. The ensuing public uproar was so great that legislators in New York and other states hastily began creating stricter safety laws for factories and other workplaces.

The Susan B. Anthony Amendment

By the time of the fire and the reforms it inspired, another major goal of the women's movement—suffrage—was finally making significant headway. By 1911, five states—Utah, Idaho, Washington, Wyoming, and Colorado—had already given women the right to vote. This trend of individual states approving female suffrage, despite the absence of a federal law allowing it, continued. In 1912, Arizona, California, Kansas, and Oregon granted women the right to vote. Two years later, Nevada and Montana followed suit.

Meanwhile, the women's rights activists who had lost momentum in the 1870s managed to regain it. In 1890, the American Woman Suffrage Association and the National Woman Suffrage Association agreed to merge. The new group was called the National American Woman Suffrage Association (NAWSA). It stepped up efforts to lobby congressmen to pass a constitutional amendment granting women's suffrage. Back in 1878, Susan B. Anthony had managed to get such an amendment introduced in Congress. It had not passed, but the amendment with the unofficial title of the "Susan B. Anthony Amendment" was reintroduced nearly every year.

Such efforts did not come without controversy. During these same years, several anti–women's suffrage organizations formed. Their members, men and women alike, were convinced that giving women the right to vote posed serious threats to society. Women's studies scholar Kathleen M. Blee explained some of their worries:

> [They] maintained that extending the vote to women would reduce the special protections and routes of influence available to women, destroy the family, and increase the number of socialist-leaning voters. These sentiments dove-tailed with the fears of many Southern whites that female suffrage would undermine the [racist] Jim Crow restrictions that effectively [kept] African American voters in the South [from casting their ballots] and the apprehension of industrial and business leaders [that] women would vote in favor of social and political reform and for prohibiting the sale of liquor.[42]

Although such groups tried their best to discredit women suffragists, the latter forged ahead and continued to call attention to their grievances. One of the most audacious examples occurred in Washington, D.C., on March 3, 1913. Led by lawyer and female rights activist Inez Milholland, who proudly rode an imposing horse, more than 5,000 women marched down Pennsylvania Avenue. Also in

HONORING SUSAN B. ANTHONY'S LEGACY

Women across the United States celebrated in 1920 when they finally received the right to vote. Women in 2018 still celebrate this right and have not forgotten the fight it took to have this right granted. November 8, 2016, was an emotional night for many women—they had received the right to vote not 100 years earlier and they were voting for the person who many believed would be the first female president, Hillary Clinton. One woman said in an interview with the *Washington Post* that she had tears in her eyes as she was filling out her ballot because of the historical significance of voting for a female president.

On election day, it is a tradition to place "I voted today" stickers on the grave of Susan B. Anthony in Rochester, New York, in thanks and recognition for her tireless efforts for woman suffrage. However, during the 2016 election day, the act of placing the sticker gained new meaning because Hillary Clinton was a major presidential candidate. Hundreds lined up to place their stickers on Anthony's grave, eventually leaving only her name visible. The line even snaked around and doubled back on itself because so many people had arrived to honor her legacy. Susan B. Anthony had been arrested for voting illegally in Rochester, but many years later, women had flocked to the same area to honor her legacy that made it acceptable to not just vote but to have the opportunity to vote for a woman. Rochester mayor Lovely Warren, who was the first woman elected to the position, said, "I was elected 141 years to the day that Susan B. Anthony cast that illegal vote … To me that means, as a woman, there are no shackles and no chains to what we can accomplish. If I could do backflips, I would be doing backflips."[1]

On November 8, 2016, people lined up at Susan B. Anthony's grave in Rochester to place their "I voted today" stickers on her grave in honor of her legacy. This act was incredibly emotional for those who attended because many had voted for a female president.

1. Quoted in Evan Real, "People Are Covering Susan B. Anthony's Gravestone with 'I Voted' Stickers," *US Magazine*, November 9, 2016. www.usmagazine.com/celebrity-news/news/people-cover-susan-b-anthonys-gravestone-with-i-voted-stickers-w449417.

Women's rights activist Inez Milholland led a crowd of women in a 1913 march in Washington, D.C. She proudly drew attention to their cause by riding a horse down Pennsylvania Avenue.

the parade were nine marching bands and about twenty-four colorful floats.

Another way that the suffragists gained attention, as well as credibility and new followers, was through their efforts to aid their country during World War I. The United States entered the conflict in April 1917. Immediately, American women rose to the challenge, bringing on a change in gender roles. World War I allowed women to step out of their normal roles, taking up positions in factories to manufacture war products such as gas masks and munitions. More than 1 million women aided in the war effort, including 90,000 who served in uniform. The U.S. Navy and Marines enlisted women for roles such as chemists, accountants, nurses, clerks, and radio electricians. The U.S. Army employed 21,000 women as fingerprint experts, translators, journalists, and clerks—it was more conservative in its jobs for women than other branches of the military.

According to the U.S. Army, before World War I, the Army Nurse Corps had 403 active-duty nurses, which rose to more than 12,180 by the end of the war in 1918. The Army Signal Corps enlisted

700 women, 332 of whom served overseas as bilingual French-speaking telephone operators. Although the Army nurses and operators were subject to the Uniform Code of Military

Justice and Army regulations and wore uniforms, they had no rank.

The Army regarded them as "civilians" employed by the War Department. It was not until the second World War that women were assigned the ranks of lieutenant or captain, and then it was only "relative rank," meaning that even though the women held all of the responsibility and respect afforded to the positions, they received far less pay and none of the benefits received by their male counterparts.[43]

At the end of the war, the women were released without recognition. Their contributions were not recognized until the Army-Navy Nurses Act in 1947. However, their "contributions did more than help America defeat her enemies. Their participation also made a powerful argument for women's voting rights, weighing heavily in the passing of the 19th Amendment giving American women the right to vote."[44]

Fighting and Winning a Revolution

In addition to their major wartime contributions, during the conflict, which ended in 1918, members of the women's movement continued their efforts to gain the vote. The leader of the NAWSA, Carrie Chapman Catt, coordinated various demonstrations and other peaceful protests with local suffrage groups across the nation. At the same time, the National Woman's Party (NWP) employed more militant means. Led by Alice Paul of New Jersey, members of the NWP picketed the White House, then viewed by most Americans as an offensive, even hostile, activity. These pickets were called the "Silent Sentinels" protests. Protesters stood outside the White House holding signs throughout 1917. More than 1,000 women from across the United States picketed outside the White House, and 218 were arrested and charged with obstructing sidewalk traffic. In addition, 97 of them were sent to Occoquan Workhouse in Virginia or to the District of Columbia jail. When pressed to explain why she approved of such tactics, Paul replied, "If a creditor stands before a man's house all day long, demanding payment of his bill, the man must either remove the creditor or pay the bill."[45]

At first, the authorities tolerated these protestors. However, as time went on, that attitude hardened, and a number of women were badly mistreated. According to researcher Deborah G. Felder,

Several months after the picketers started their silent White House vigil, the police began making arrests. The picketers, who had been demonstrating legally, were set free without sentence—at first. When they returned to the picket lines, they were arrested on a charge of obstructing sidewalk traffic, found guilty, and imprisoned in the [Occoquan] workhouse in Virginia. There Alice Paul, journalist Dorothy Day, and other picketers went on a hunger strike and were force-fed. Paul, whose hunger strike lasted twenty-two days, was considered insane by prison officials and forced to undergo a mental examination.[46]

These abuses culminated in what came to be known as the "Night of Terror." The male prison guards went on a rampage, beating and choking the women and leaving those they had injured in their cells with no medical treatment. When word of what had happened reached the public, there was widespread outrage. The courts pronounced most of the arrests invalid, and not long afterward, the prisoners gained their freedom.

While the drama of the imprisoned NWP members was unfolding, the NAWSA stepped up its pressure on congressmen, urging them to pass the Susan B. Anthony Amendment. Its members also lobbied the president, Woodrow Wilson, at every turn. Eventually, he came around, agreed to back the bill, and began winning over legislators behind the scenes. As a result, on January 10, 1918, after many years of rejecting the amendment, the House of Representatives passed it. The vote was

274–136, which achieved the two-thirds majority required to adopt a constitutional amendment.

All eyes now fell on the U.S. Senate, which also had to approve the bill for it to become law. There, to the suffragists' disappointment, the vote tally did not attain the needed two-thirds majority. Undaunted, the suffragists, still backed by the president, kept up their pressure on the senators, a strategy that worked. On June 4, 1919, the Senate voted again on the Anthony Amendment, which had now come to be called the 19th Amendment. This time, the bill passed by a vote of 56–25.

In the next and final stage in the process, the legislation went to the states. Three-quarters of them had to ratify it for it to become law, a procedure that took a little more than a year. On August 24, 1920, the deciding state, Tennessee, mailed its certificate of ratification to Washington, D.C. When it arrived at the Capitol building on August 26, the U.S. secretary of state announced that the 19th Amendment had officially become part of the U.S. Constitution. Susan B. Anthony, however, never got to see the amendment she fought so hard for get ratified—she had died in 1906 of pneumonia.

Seventy-two years after a small meeting in upstate New York had set the women's movement in motion, a truly momentous victory had been achieved, and one that women still celebrate today. At the NAWSA's Washington office, Carrie Chapman Catt told her staff, "It was a great crusade; the world has seen none more wonderful ... My admiration, love, and reverence go out to that band [of women who] fought and won a revolution, [with] congratulations that we were permitted to establish a new and good thing in the world."[47] In 1920, NAWSA's name was also changed to the League of Women Voters, with the new goal of training women to become good citizens.

CHAPTER FOUR

FIGHTING FOR ACCEPTANCE AND RESPECT

With the long-awaited victory of the passage of the 19th Amendment, not only did women take advantage of their new freedom to also run for public offices, but a new identity also emerged. Women had the right to vote, and they also felt free to break away from the typical roles that women held in previous generations. They danced in public, drank alcohol, wore their hair in short bobs, and regularly wore makeup—they were able to freely express themselves as men had always been able to. This new social image that emerged was referred to as a flapper. A flapper was generally fun-loving, carefree, and mirrored the positive outlook of the 1920s, which was called the Roaring Twenties or the Jazz Age. As nightclubs opened and jazz concerts were performed, these women fully embraced their identity and demanded to participate in these leisurely activities with men.

With the emergence of a new, freer identity, strong female role models also emerged who took on the role of representing women and fighting for acceptance and respect. The winning of one battle did not mean women were done fighting—the ultimate goal was equal rights.

Women Must Continue to Assert Themselves

Whether a woman in the Roaring Twenties was well-off or poor, she still had certain rights that the women of her mother's generation had fought hard to acquire, such as the right to vote. Many of the former suffragists and other activists were content with this level of progress and felt that their work was largely done.

The NWP, still led by Alice Paul,

Zelda Fitzgerald (center) was a novelist, painter, and female icon of the Roaring Twenties. Her husband, F. Scott Fitzgerald (left), was a famous novelist and chronicler of the era. His most famous book is The Great Gatsby.

THE ERA

The original draft of the Equal Rights Amendment, or ERA, was written by Alice Paul in 1921, shortly after the ratification of the 19th Amendment. She introduced the new document to her colleagues at a 1923 commemoration of the 1848 Seneca Falls Convention. Then informally called the "Lucretia Mott Amendment," its core sentiment stated, "Men and women shall have equal rights throughout the United States and every place subject to its jurisdiction."[1] This wording was later changed somewhat, and the version of the bill that eventually passed Congress reads as follows:

> Section 1. Equality of rights under the law shall not be denied or abridged by the United States or by any state on account of sex.

> Section 2. The Congress shall have the power to enforce, by appropriate legislation, the provisions of this article.

> Section 3. This amendment shall take effect two years after the date of ratification.[2]

1. Quoted in Roberta W. Francis, "The History Behind the Equal Rights Amendment," Alice Paul Institute, accessed January 12, 2018. www.equalrightsamendment.org/history.htm.
2. Francis, "The History Behind the Equal Rights Amendment."

was less satisfied, however. Paul and her colleagues felt that gaining the vote had been an important step but that women were still far from equal and must continue to assert themselves.

The chief tool the NWP chose to attain the goal of full equality was another constitutional amendment, which became known as the Equal Rights Amendment (ERA). Written by Paul, it stated that men and women should have equal rights in all the United States and its territories. The use of the broad term "rights," as opposed to naming specific rights, was intended to be an umbrella term to cover all rights, including legal ones. Opponents feared that giving women legal equality with men would force employers to provide equal pay for women and end other forms of discrimination against women. Despite widespread opposition, the NWP

The ERA has not been ratified as of 2018. Shown here is a rally in Washington, D.C., protesting the fact that the amendment had been passed but still not ratified.

persevered and in 1923 managed to secure a congressional hearing on the amendment. However, at the time, no one realized that it would be several decades before Congress would decide to pass it. It would not pass Congress until 1972, at which point it was sent to the states for ratification. However, only 35 out of the required 38 states ratified it before the 7-year deadline in 1982. It has been introduced at every Congress since then, and as of 2018, it still has not been ratified.

Partly because the ERA was rejected in the 1920s, the struggle for expanded rights in the women's movement declined in that decade. Another reason was that the U.S. War Department suspected wrongly that many women's organizations were pacifistic (anti-war) and had ties to communism. That dissuaded numerous women from joining these groups. In addition, women's unions virtually disappeared, making it more difficult for female workers to fight inequality in the workplace.

In the years directly following the passage of the 19th Amendment, therefore, women made little headway in political, legal, or labor rights. The only significant improvement in their status was their increased acceptance by most men in various social and public spheres and situations, which did prove to be a major and permanent advancement.

Emergence of Strong Role Models

In the years following the passage of the 19th Amendment, a small group of elite women emerged who broke new ground and are still role models for many. Several of these women had earlier worked as suffragists and knew how to organize and work toward solving problems and achieving goals. It was from their ranks that President Franklin D. Roosevelt chose women such as Frances Perkins to help create new government policies to deal with the economic crisis of the Great Depression. Perkins became instrumental in fashioning the Social Security program, for example. It provided badly needed aid to older women and men from 1935 on and remains a government safety net for elderly Americans today. Another of Roosevelt's appointees, Mary McLeod Bethune, ran the Office of Minority Affairs for the National Youth Administration. She also had the distinction of being the first African American to head a U.S. government agency. Bethune was a highly intelligent, hardworking, and determined individual. She proved that even in the face of entrenched racism and sexism, a woman of her talents could rise to a position of influence in a country that was slowly but steadily shedding its long-standing biases against females.

The most widely known and respected woman in Depression-era

Eleanor Roosevelt is the most widely known and respected woman who lived during the Depression era. Many women were inspired to receive a college education because of her.

The chief visual image of Rosie the Riveter, the fictional character who became a symbol of American female industrial workers during World War II, was a painting by artist J. Howard Miller. It showed a woman with brown hair rolling up her sleeve (an action representing getting to work) and simultaneously flexing her right bicep, a typically male gesture. The image was part of a series of posters commissioned by the Westinghouse Company and created by Miller to support the war effort. Another famous image of "Rosie" was illustrated by artist Norman Rockwell for the cover of the *Saturday Evening Post* in May 1943. As part of a propaganda effort, government officials located other "Rosies" across the country—women who were photographed in poses mimicking the one in the paintings—and employed them in various media ads.

Naomi Parker-Fraley was the inspiration behind the Rosie the Riveter poster, shown here. Parker-Fraley died in January 2018.

America was First Lady Eleanor Roosevelt. A strong supporter of women's causes, she urged her husband to utilize the talents of as many women as possible. She also made sure that women who had workable ideas for government programs were granted access to the White House and members of the president's cabinet. In addition, she allowed only female reporters to cover her own news conferences. This forced every news outlet that desired to cover the White House to hire at least one woman. In turn, a number of other young women were inspired to seek college educations and careers in journalism.

World War II

As the 1930s gave way to the next decade, many American women suddenly found themselves with unexpected opportunities to work and contribute to society in new ways. The United States entered World War II the day after Japanese planes bombed the American military bases at Pearl Harbor in Hawai'i on December 7, 1941. Millions of American men quickly enlisted, creating an enormous labor shortage. To fill their places, large numbers of women rose to the challenge as they did in previous wars. Once again, they worked in factories making war-related products and other materials. The rest worked as waitresses and secretaries.

The women who took jobs in factories, many of which made guns, airplanes, tanks, jeeps, and other war machines, were particularly important to the war effort. Both to attract women to such jobs and to celebrate their patriotism and capabilities, the government sponsored propaganda campaigns. The most famous featured the tough, proud fictional character Rosie the Riveter.

Unfortunately for African American women, they were sorely underutilized in the war, primarily because of overt racism, which was still rampant in American society. Some service branches did accept a few black women, but they were segregated from white women. This did not prevent them from disproving their supposed inferiority by serving with distinction.

Indeed, the outstanding performance of women in both industry and the military during the war became an important factor in changing social attitudes about women. In turn, that led to their increased acceptance in the workplace in the postwar years. In fact, many historians credit women's wide-ranging work experiences between 1941 and 1945 with partially motivating a revival of the women's movement in the 1960s.

World War II had given millions of American women the chance to work outside the home, many of them for the first time. However, these opportunities did not become an automatic springboard for women's continued social advancement after the conflict. Instead, society's postwar expectations for women seemed to revert to the traditional notion that they primarily belonged in the home, and even though women wanted to keep their jobs, they lost them to veterans returning from the war.

"EDUCATION IS THE KEY TO EFFECTIVE PARTICIPATION"

The following excerpt from the National Organization for Women's statement of purpose, drafted in 1966, calls for allowing women to become as well educated as the best-educated men:

> We believe that it is as essential for every girl to be educated to her full potential of human ability as it is for every boy—with the knowledge that such education is the key to effective participation in today's economy and that, for a girl as for a boy, education can only be serious where there is expectation that it will be used in society … We consider the decline in the proportion of women receiving higher and professional education to be evidence of discrimination. This discrimination may take the form of quotas against the admission of women to colleges and professional schools; lack of encouragement by parents, counselors, and educators; [or] denial of loans or fellowships. [We] believe that the same serious attention must be given to high school dropouts who are girls as to boys.[1]

1. Quoted in Betty Friedan, *It Changed My Life: Writings on the Women's Movement*. New York, NY: Random House, 1976, p. 89.

Platforms for a New Women's Movement

Women felt that the stay-at-home mother image of American women so prevalent in the 1950s was outdated and unfair. They argued that large numbers of women either had to work to support themselves and their families or desired to have their own careers in addition to or instead of their role as housewives. However, stigmas against such female independence still remained. Additionally, those women who did work still did not receive equal treatment in the workplace, demonstrated by the reality that they earned considerably less than men for performing the same jobs. Many women felt that it was only fair that society address such gender-related inequities.

These rising grievances motivated a few influential women, notably Assistant Secretary of Labor Esther Peterson, to approach President John F. Kennedy shortly after he took office in 1961. They urged him to establish what became known as the

Presidential Commission on the Status of Women. He did so that year, asking the group's members to determine where women stood in society and to suggest ways in which their situation might be improved.

The commission issued its report, titled "American Women," in 1963. It detailed serious anti-female discrimination in employment, including unequal pay, lack of child care and other social services, inequality in education, and various forms of legal inequality. On the basis of these findings, the president immediately ordered two important reforms. First, he required that hiring for all civil service, or government, jobs must be done "solely on the basis of ability to meet the requirements of the position, and without regard to [biological] sex."[48]

Kennedy also pushed the Equal Pay Act (EPA) through Congress. The new law banned employers from paying women less than men for the same work. Although the EPA was spottily enforced and did not eradicate unequal pay practices, its overall effect was positive. When it passed in 1963, women made about 59 cents for each dollar a man made for the same job. By 1970, that ratio had risen to 62 cents per dollar.

Although Kennedy's reforms were helpful, concerned women felt that many more reforms were needed. For that to happen, American women needed to be well-informed about the problems they faced. They also needed to effectively organize and lobby for new reforms in the same way the suffragists had in the century's early decades. To these ends, in the same year the EPA passed, noted writer and activist Betty Friedan published her book *The Feminine Mystique*. It detailed how women had been largely relegated to the home in the years following World War II and called attention to the many social inequalities women were still forced to deal with.

In addition, in 1966, Friedan established the National Organization for Women (NOW). It provided American women with a group that could fight for their rights through the media, the courts, and Congress. NOW's initial statement of intent began, "The purpose of NOW is to take action to bring women into full participation in the mainstream of American society now, exercising all the privileges and responsibilities thereof in truly equal partnership with men."[49] In some ways, NOW was a modern version of the 1848 Seneca Falls Convention, that is, a platform to support a women's rights movement. NOW members pushed for passage of the ERA and abortion rights, urged strong enforcement of existing federal laws against discrimination, and organized public protests against gender discrimination. Thanks to these and other organized activities designed to further

President John F. Kennedy helped women win additional victories by establishing the Commission on the Status of Women and pushing the Equal Pay Act through Congress. He is shown here at the ceremony for the signing of the Equal Pay Act.

women's equality, NOW and other similar organizations rapidly gained new members. The growing new women's movement did not reach or inspire every female American, but those it did reach felt their lives were changed for the better. In 1967 a recent Harvard University graduate named Sara Ruddick wrote in her diary that

the women's movement enabled me to achieve a new self-respect at home, made me confident and clear about my need for the friendship of women. [Before] I had carried an invisible, almost amorphous [shapeless] weight, the weight of guilt and apology for [having] interests and ambitions that should have been a source of pride [but that some men

said women should not be doing].
When that weight was lifted, I felt
almost literally lighter, certainly
more energetic, more concentrated.[50]

Women's Liberation

By 1970, the main thrust of the new women's movement was popularly known by the shorthand term "women's lib" (short for "liberation"). Women who had the time and energy did their part for the cause by taking part in marches, writing or calling their congressional representatives, and making monetary contributions to women's organizations. Among average, non-activist women, meanwhile, some were big supporters of the movement and were pleased when they heard about strides made by organizations such as NOW.

Whether one agreed or disagreed with the women's movement and its activism, no one doubted that it was having a growing effect on society. Women made increasingly bold statements, both in writing and in public. On March 18, 1970, 100 women staged a sit-in at the New York City offices of the *Ladies' Home Journal* and for 11 hours engaged its editor John Mack Carter and his assistants in fervent debate. A magazine that claimed to support women, the protestors said, should pay its female employees a living wage. It should also provide day care for its employees and hire more minorities. Carter listened intently and agreed to publish an eight-page account of the event and the demonstrators' demands in that year's August issue. He stated in the account,

Beneath the shrill accusations and the radical dialectic [argument], our editors heard some convincing truths about the persistence of sexual discrimination in many areas of American life. [We] seemed to catch a rising note of angry self-expression among today's American women, a desire for representation, for recognition, for a broadening range of alternatives [in their lives].[51]

The supportive statements Carter made about women's lib resonated with special force because the August issue in which they appeared coincided with the 50th anniversary of the passage of the 19th Amendment in 1920. To hammer the message home even harder, a few days later, on August 26, NOW sponsored a Women's Strike for Equality. Tens of thousands of women marched and protested in cities and towns across the nation. These demonstrations were so effective that in the weeks and months that followed, the membership of NOW chapters in all corners of the country swelled. Meanwhile, feminists from NOW and other women's organizations stepped up their lobbying and educational efforts. They wrote books and magazine articles,

About 100 women staged a sit-in at the Ladies' Home Journal *offices in 1970.*

went on TV and radio talk shows, and lectured at colleges and local community gatherings.

Pro-Women Developments

The visibility and influence of the women's movement expanded as it never had before. In the ensuing two years, a series of dramatic events propelled women's rights issues into the forefront of American life, conversation, debate, and legislative and legal decisions. In 1971, for instance, Betty Friedan, Congresswomen Bella Abzug and Shirley Chisholm, journalist Gloria Steinem, and several other leading feminists established the National Women's Political Caucus (NWPC). It was a bipartisan organization, meaning that it was open to members of both major political parties. One goal of the NWPC was to recruit and train feminist-minded women for government offices. Another was to help them get elected or appointed to those offices. The office holders then proceeded to lobby hard for various social and political objectives, including better education for women, legislation banning discrimination against women, and passage of the ERA.

Gloria Steinem was instrumental in creating another powerful tool to advance women's causes in that same year. She became the publisher and editor of a new magazine called *Ms.* This term had been recently coined by feminists to replace Miss and Mrs., which indicate marital status. Since men were addressed by just one term—Mr.—which does not reveal said status, feminists felt that, in fairness, women should also be addressed by an equally nonjudgmental term. The first national feminist magazine, *Ms.* carried articles dealing with women's issues, among them abortion rights, domestic violence, equality in the workplace, and many more. The magazine, which premiered in January 1972, was an instant and huge success. The first 300,000 copies sold out in just 8 days. As of 2018, the magazine is still being published.

The early 1970s also witnessed a flurry of national legislation designed to ensure more gender equality in the country. In 1972, Congress passed and President Richard M. Nixon signed into law the Equal Employment Opportunity Act. Among other things, it created the Equal Employment Opportunity Commission (EEOC). The EEOC investigates claims submitted to it that some sort of discrimination has occurred in the workplace. If the agency determines reasonable cause for the claim, it can sue the employer in a federal court.

Nixon also signed an educational bill best known as Title IX. It bans discrimination in all educational institutions that receive federal money. Many such schools had earlier maintained limits on the number of women they accepted in certain programs. The effect of the new law, which eliminated these limits, was dramatic. In 1972, 9 percent of medical degrees in the country were earned by women, compared to 38 percent in 1994. Experts credited much of the increase to Title IX. The law also requires that schools receiving federal funds offer women equal opportunities to play sports as those offered to men.

Also in 1972, under intense lobbying by women's groups, Congress passed the Equal Rights Amendment. This was seen as a major victory, especially considering that the bill's opponents had lobbied just as hard to stop it. Still another event that feminists viewed as a victory occurred in 1973. In the case *Roe v. Wade*, the U.S. Supreme Court ruled that a woman could not be denied the right to an abortion performed during the first trimester of pregnancy. The decision was and still is viewed as highly controversial.

However, at the time, it seemed to cap the stunning series of pro-women developments of the previous two years. Women had found new roles and greater respect in the workplace. They had also gained a greater voice in government, expanded educational opportunities, and the right to decide for themselves whether a pregnancy should or should not be terminated. Overall, feminist concerns and organizations were now a regular and permanent part of the American social and political scene. This would ensure that positive change would continue in the future, even if slowly.

CHAPTER FIVE

STEPS TOWARD FEMALE EQUALITY

With the failure of the states to ratify the ERA, organizations that had been fighting for women's rights for years continued their fight, and many changes occurred in women's lives. Things that were off limits to them before were now opened up for them. Women were able to advance in the typically masculine military to positions such as four-star general. In addition, women were assigned to more political roles, allowing other women to feel like they had representation in government.

Making Oneself Heard

This continuing struggle to improve the status and rights women remains a slow, though steady, process. A major reason that it occurs at what some feminists have complained is a very gradual rate is that social change of any kind always has its opponents. In every era, large segments of society tend to resist attempts to modify accepted traditions, especially when those modifications seem at first glance to be too radical.

A majority of feminists feel that this is why opposition to the ERA has been so great. In their view, some Americans felt threatened by the empowerment of women. These Americans worried that the amendment would bring about social changes that might adversely affect traditional morality and the established social order. Such worries for society's well-being are illustrated by the writings of the late Baptist preacher Jerry Falwell, who amassed a large following of concerned Americans in the 1980s and 1990s. He condemned both the ERA and the modern women's movement itself as threats to both society and Christian tradition, saying,

Feminists are saying that self-satisfaction is more important than the family. Most of the women who

are leaders in the feminist movement promote an immoral lifestyle. In a drastic departure from the home, more than half of the women in our country are currently employed. Our nation is in serious danger when motherhood is considered a task that is "unrewarding, unfulfilling, and boring." I believe that a woman's calling to be a wife and mother is the highest calling in the world ... The Equal Rights Amendment is a delusion. [It] can never do for women what needs to be done for them. Women need ... a man who knows Jesus Christ as his Lord and Savior, and they need to be part of a home where their husband is a godly leader.[52]

Many Americans agreed with Falwell and other critics of the women's movement. They said that they were not against women's rights to self-expression and fulfillment. Rather, they felt that many of the feminists' demands and proposed reforms were too radical. Few doubt that these sentiments were partially responsible for the ERA's defeat, as well as for strong opposition to numerous other reforms advocated in the decades that followed.

However, women persevered. Despite many obstacles, they managed to improve their social status, even when their advances were slow and incremental. This happened in part because they explored new ways of making themselves heard and instigating change. As historian Nancy MacLean wrote,

Feminist organizing continued and even reached into new [social] arenas. As the direct action phase of the movement waned, women brought feminist ideas into the range of institutions that made up American society and reshaped them ... A cohort [group] of younger women set out to update feminism to meet the challenge of new conditions. The first generation born in the wake of the women's movement's greatest victories came of age in the 1990s, when the contradictions of the women's movement's unfinished revolution were startlingly apparent in American life. They focused on issues of pressing concern to them, such as ... self-image, diversity, [the] balance [between work and family, and] voter registration campaigns to draw young women into politics.[53]

Year of the Woman

The last issue MacLean mentioned—drawing more women into the political arena—is a crucial step toward female equality.

A significant example in the United States occurred in 1984. New York lawyer Geraldine Ferraro became the first woman nominated for vice president by a major U.S. party when the Democrats chose her as the running mate to Walter Mondale (who opposed Ronald Reagan for the presidency).

Although the Democrats lost the election, Ferraro's candidacy became a symbol of changing times for women in politics. More and more women were inspired to run for public offices of all kinds. Some lost their races, but increasing numbers won them, a trend that culminated in 1992, which became known as the "Year of the Woman." More female candidates were elected that year than in any prior year. They included 19 congresswomen, raising the number of women in the House of Representatives to 47; and 3 senators, bringing the number of women in the Senate to 7. One of these new senators, Carol Moseley Braun, was the first black woman ever to serve in the Senate.

These political gains set the stage for even more stunning triumphs for women in the two decades that followed. In 2007, congresswoman Nancy Pelosi of California became the first female speaker of the House of Representatives. That put her second, after the vice president, in the line of succession activated in the event the president cannot finish his term in office.

The following year, Democrat Hillary Rodham Clinton became the first U.S. woman to win a presidential primary (in New Hampshire). Running against her fellow Democratic candidates, she received an impressive 18 million votes in the primary season. Although Barack Obama narrowly defeated her in the primaries and went on to be elected the first African American U.S. president, he appointed Clinton to the prestigious post of secretary of state early in 2009. Meanwhile, during the same presidential election, Sarah Palin, governor of Alaska, was the first woman nominated for vice president by the Republican Party (running with Senator John McCain, who lost to Obama).

Strides were also made by women in appointed government positions, most notably the Supreme Court. In 1981, President Reagan nominated Arizona judge Sandra Day O'Connor to the high court, and the U.S. Senate confirmed her unanimously. She provided the swing vote in many cases, making her one of the most influential of the nine justices on the court. Other female appointments to the Supreme Court followed. They include Ruth Bader Ginsburg, who was appointed in 1993 and became the second female justice; Sonia Sotomayor in 2009; and Elena Kagan in 2010. When Kagan took her seat on the court, for the first time in U.S. history it featured three women, making up a third of the justices.

Women in the Military
Barriers that held women back continued to fall in the 1990s,

Hillary Clinton made history by becoming the first woman to win a presidential primary in the United States. She had a large group of supporters, but Barack Obama defeated her, going on to become the first African American U.S. president.

especially in the military. According to Nancy MacLean,

> Participants in the Defense Advisory Committee on Women in the Armed Forces pressed [the Defense Department] successfully to integrate the armed forces [with female soldiers] and make the [military authorities] act on sexual harassment and other forms of discrimination against servicewomen. The changes proved especially important to African American women and Latinas, who enlist in the military in large numbers in hopes of education funding and social mobility.[54]

The effects of the increased

President Barack Obama is shown here signing the Lilly Ledbetter Fair Pay Act into law. Ledbetter (second from right) was at the signing of this historic law.

for women's human rights has just begun. As each generation shares its secrets, women learn to see the world through their own eyes, and discover, much to their surprise, that they are not the first, and that they are not alone. [A] revolution is under way, and there is no end in sight."[55]

PERSEVERANCE IN THE FACE OF OPPOSITION

Emma Watson—actress, feminist, and Global Goodwill Ambassador of UN Women—once said, "Women and girls have always faced hurdles. But that's never stopped us. We've sacrificed, fought, campaigned, succeeded, been knocked back, and succeeded again. In a race for justice, we've leapt over countless obstacles to win our rights."[56] While great strides have been made through the past centuries, there is still much that has not changed. While women's rights have come a long way since the time that Susan B. Anthony, Elizabeth Cady Stanton, and Alice Paul were fighting for them, there is still much to be done. This continuing inequity was made visible on January 21, 2017, with the various women's marches, which were events that had risen from ongoing concerns about immigration, reproductive rights, LGBT+ rights, civil rights, and more. Women in 2017 were following in the footsteps of the strong, influential women who had done the same so many years ago, and just like those women, there is no sign of stopping until full, equal rights are achieved.

U.S. Presidential Campaign of 2016

Women had fought for their rights for hundreds of years, and change was very gradual. When Hillary Clinton announced she was running for U.S. president in the 2016 election, many felt hopeful. History was made years earlier with the first African American president, and many thought it would be made again with the first woman president. Women have been struggling with achieving full equality with men for many years, and there is still a large gap between the incomes of men and women. With a female president, many thought that there would be more equality for all groups, including all races and the LGBT+ community. In addition, marginalized groups felt like they would have a voice, and it could maybe inspire

The women's marches held on January 21, 2017, were not the first marches held for women's rights. These marchers were following in the footsteps of women who fought for the same rights many years before and are still fighting for a revolution.

others from these groups to run for office themselves as there would be a precedent set with the first African American president and first woman president.

The major candidates in the 2016 presidential election were Hillary Clinton and Donald Trump. Clinton had 31 years of government experience, and her campaign platform included:

- free tuition at public colleges for in-state students of families who made less than $125,000 per year
- immigration reform
- affordable health care
- equal pay
- keeping middle-class taxes as they were and not raising them
- increasing the federal minimum wage
- expanding background checks for gun sales to cut down on gun violence
- increasing funding for things such as maintaining bridges, highways, and airports

Donald Trump came to the presidential election without government experience, and his campaign platform was unconventional. Some of his promises included:

- building a wall on the border between the United States and Mexico and making Mexico pay for the wall
- banning Muslims from entering the United States
- bringing back manufacturing jobs
- repealing the Affordable Care Act (also called "Obamacare" by some)

Election Day 2016

Considering Clinton's extensive government experience and the scope of her campaign platform, many believed she was going to be elected the first female U.S. president. However, at the

HeForShe

In 2014, United Nations (UN) Women created the gender equality campaign called HeForShe. Its goal is for every voice to be heard because every person has a role to play in achieving gender equality. HeForShe focuses on the empowerment of women and

Emma Watson is an important activist for gender equality and is also a Global Goodwill Ambassador of UN Women.

provides a systematic approach and targeted platform on which men and boys can engage and become change agents towards the achievement of gender equality. Achieving gender equality in our lifetimes requires an innovative, inclusive approach that both recognizes men and boys as partners for women's rights, and acknowledges the ways in which they also benefit from this equality.[1]

Harry Potter actress Emma Watson is one of the most vocal supporters of the HeForShe campaign, an activist for gender equality, and the Global Goodwill Ambassador of UN Women. At the launch of the HeForShe campaign, Watson said, "How can we affect change in the world when only half of it is invited or feel welcome to participate in the conversation?"[2] Watson is one of the major celebrity voices in the fight for gender equality, and she participated in the Women's March on Washington in 2017. Her role in this fight is even more powerful because she is one of the biggest movie stars in the world and a household name from her role in the *Harry Potter* series, which is one of the largest and most popular movie and book franchises of all time.

1. "HeForShe: In Brief," HeForShe, accessed January 15, 2018. www.heforshe.org/-/media/heforshe/files/our%20mission/heforshe_overview_brief.pdf?la=en.
2. "Emma Watson: Gender Equality Is Your Issue Too," UN Women, September 20, 2014. www.unwomen.org/en/news/stories/2014/9/emma-watson-gender-equality-is-your-issue-too.

end of Election Day, it was announced that Donald Trump would be the 45th president of the United States. Clinton won the popular vote with 65,853,516 votes, while Trump had 62,984,825 votes—there were more votes for Clinton than any other losing presidential candidate in the history of the United States. However, what determines the president of the United States is the electoral college vote. The electoral vote consists of 538 electors, with the majority of 270 being needed to elect the next president. Trump won the electoral vote with 306 votes, and Clinton had 232.

Election Day 2016 created concern for many feminists based on remarks that Trump had made in the past and while on the campaign trail. He said many things about specific women

Hillary Clinton made history by losing the presidential election with more popular votes than any other losing president in U.S. history. This showed that many Americans were ready to elect a female president.

and women in general, including that certain women were unattractive, that women who got abortions should be punished, and that women could be grabbed inappropriately without their consent. Other remarks he made were directed at Clinton and her status as a female candidate, including that "the only card [Hillary Clinton] has is the woman's card ... she's got nothing else to offer and frankly, if Hillary Clinton were a man, I don't think she'd get 5 percent of the vote. The only thing she's got going is the woman's card, and the beautiful thing is, women don't like her."[57]

The Women's March

Clinton winning the popular vote but not the electoral vote created concern that birthed a new revolution. Upon finding out the election results, Teresa Shook did something about the sadness she felt from the results. She created a Facebook event page that called for a march on Washington, D.C. Before she went to bed, there were 40 responses for the event—when she woke up, there were 10,000. On November 10, fashion designer Bob Bland responded to the Facebook event and wrote, "I think we should build a coalition of ALL marginalized allies + do this ... We will need folks from every state + city to organize their communities locally, who wants to join me?"[58]

Bland then consolidated Shook's and other protest pages and recruited three activists—Tamika Mallory, Carmen Perez, and Linda Sarsour—to be chairs of the national march. Mallory is a gun-control advocate, Perez is head of a criminal-justice reform group, and Sarsour led a successful campaign for public schools in New York City to be closed on Muslim holidays. These women had experience organizing campaigns and brought this experience to a movement that was rapidly gaining traction. The organizers chose the name Women's March on Washington after Martin Luther King Jr.'s 1963 civil rights march, the March on Washington for Jobs and Freedom.

The small idea for a movement quickly grew. About 2 million people around the world marched in demonstrations in their own cities or traveled to the largest march in Washington, D.C. The people who marched had concerns over women's rights issues, but they were also concerned about issues involving LGBT+ rights, climate change concerns, and racism. Marchers carried signs with quotes from people such as Martin Luther King Jr. or signs with reasons why they were there. One person who participated said they felt better after marching because they were with a group of people who felt the same as they did—the movement has provided a community for people who celebrate diversity. Others said they felt hopeful. Sanjay Sabnani said, "As the father of three amazing young women, the son of an incredible mother, and the friend of so many others, I am saddened that they still have to fight for logic and

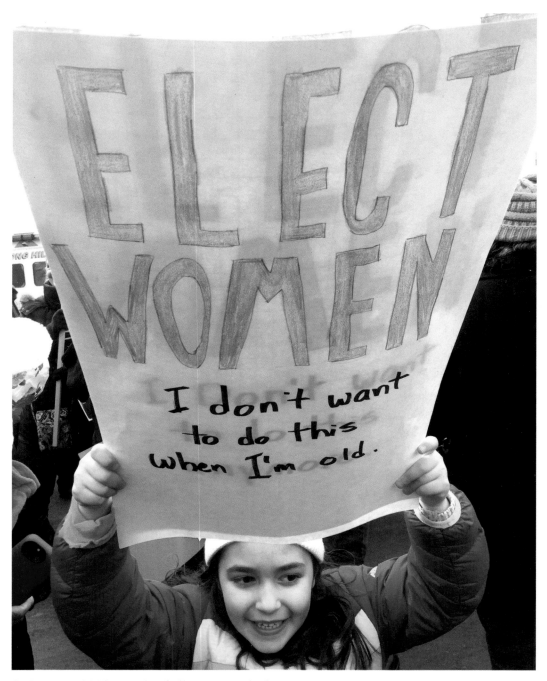

In January 2018, people of all ages marched in various one-year anniversary demonstrations of the Women's March on Washington. A young activist at a march in New Jersey is shown here.

decency. I took my daughter to the march to let her know that it is always OK to stand up for what you believe in and because I want her to know that I believe in her."[59]

While the idea for the march grew into hundreds of marches, it also grew into an organization that continues to fight for change. In addition, anniversary marches have been held to show that women and marginalized groups will not back down until there is full equality. In 2018, the Women's March gathered in Las Vegas, Nevada, for the next event, which was Women's March: Power to the Polls, which launched a national voter registration tour. The purpose of the tour was to register even more voters to bring about further social change. As ancestors have shown in the earliest days of the women's movement, the way to bring about change is to have representatives in government.

The way to make this happen is to vote, and not just for the president—it is incredibly important to vote in each election and be fully informed about each candidate, even in small elections because these are the people who help bring about change.

At the time of the Women's March: Power to the Polls, women had the right to vote for 98 years. It was a right that some who fought the hardest for never got to see happen. The Women's March is carrying on in the footsteps of its ancestors, showing that sometimes a small idea can bring about worldwide change. As Hillary Clinton said at the Women in the World Summit in 2012, "We need to be as fearless as the women whose stories you have applauded, as committed as the dissidents and the activists you have heard from, as [bold] as those who start movements for peace when all seems lost."[60]

Notes

Introduction:
"Women's Rights Are Human Rights"

1. Quoted in Amy Chozick, "Hillary Clinton's Beijing Speech on Women Resonates 20 Years Later," *New York Times*, September 5, 2015. www.nytimes.com/politics/first-draft/2015/09/05/20-years-later-hillary-clintons-beijing-speech-on-women-resonates.

2. Elizabeth K. Minnich, "Education," in *The Reader's Companion to U.S. Women's History*, eds. Wilma Mankiller et al. Boston, MA: Houghton Mifflin, 1998, p. 166.

3. Sara M. Evans, *Born for Liberty: A History of Women in America*. New York, NY: Free Press, 1989, p. 314.

4. Quoted in Tamara Keith, "Sexism Is Out in the Open in the 2016 Campaign. That May Have Been Inevitable," NPR, October 23, 2016. www.npr.org/2016/10/23/498878356/sexism-is-out-in-the-open-in-the-2016-campaign-that-may-have-been-inevitable.

5. Quoted in Alejandra Maria Salazar, "Organizers Hope Women's March on Washington Inspires, Evolves," NPR, December 21, 2016. www.npr.org/2016/12/21/506299560/womens-march-on-washington-aims-to-be-more-than-protest-but-will-it.

Chapter One:
Second-Class Citizens

6. Quoted in J. K. Hosmer, ed., *John Winthrop's Journal, 1630–1649, vol. 2*. New York, NY: Scribner's, 1908, p. 239.

7. Eleanor Flexner and Ellen Fitzpatrick, *Century of Struggle: The Women's Rights Movement in the United States*. Cambridge, MA: Harvard University Press, 1996, p. 8.

8. Julie Richter, "Women in Colonial Virginia," *Encyclopedia Virginia*, last updated November 21, 2013. www.encyclopediavirginia.org/Women_in_Colonial_Virginia#start_entry.

For More Information

Books

Bausum, Ann. *With Courage and Cloth: Winning the Fight for a Woman's Right to Vote*. Des Moines, IA: National Geographic, 2004.
    This book features photographs, some of which were never published before, and information on the fight for voting rights.

Friedan, Betty. *The Feminine Mystique*. New York, NY: W. W. Norton & Company, 2013.
    This essential text on feminism sparked the modern wave of the women's movement.

Pankhurst, Sylvia. *The Suffragette: The History of the Women's Militant Suffrage Movement*. Mineola, NY: Dover Publications, 2015.
    Pankhurst's book details the fight for woman's suffrage in Europe. She details the tactics of the protesters and their motives, as well as the consequences of their actions.

Wellman, Judith. *The Road to Seneca Falls: Elizabeth Cady Stanton and the First Woman's Rights Convention*. Champaign, IL: University of Illinois Press, 2004.
    This book details the fight for voting rights and the Seneca Falls Convention.

Women's March Organizers and Conde Nast. *Together We Rise: Behind the Scenes at the Protest Heard Around the World*. New York, NY: Dey Street Books, 2018.
    This full-color book features photos from the Women's March on January 21, 2017, and has numerous essays by feminist activists.

Websites

"The Fight for Women's Suffrage"
www.history.com/topics/womens-history/the-fight-for-womens-suffrage
   This article examines the long fight for suffrage.

HeForShe
www.heforshe.org/en
   This UN Women organization fights for gender equality and has information
   on how it is bringing about change, as well as how others can take action.

"The Original Women's March on Washington and the Suffragists Who Paved the Way"
www.smithsonianmag.com/history/original-womens-march-washington-and-
suffragists-who-paved-way-180961869
   This article has information on the beginning of the women's movement and
   how the actions these women took influenced the movement of the 2000s.

Women's March
www.womensmarch.com
   The official website of the Women's March, this website has information on
   the movement as well as upcoming events. (Always ask a parent or guardian
   before participating in events.)

The Women's Movement
www.pbslearningmedia.org/collection/the-womens-movement/#.
WlzrWCOZNmA
   This PBS website has extensive information on the various waves of the
   women's movement.

Index

Picture Credits

Cover Kyodo News via Getty Images; pp. 6–7 Aaron P. Bernstein/Getty Images; pp. 6 (left), 17 North Wind Picture Archives; pp. 6 (center, right), 24–25, 33, 38, 56–57 Courtesy of the Library of Congress; p. 7 (left) George Rinhart/Corbis via Getty Images; p. 7 (right) 3000ad/Shutterstock.com; p. 9 Harry Hu/Shutterstock.com; p. 10 Luca Teuchmann/WireImage/Getty Images; p. 12 ANDREW CABALLERO-REYNOLDS/AFP/Getty Images; pp. 14, 22 Courtesy of the New York Public Library; p. 19 Courtesy of the American Antiquarian Society, Worcester, Massachusetts; p. 29 Chip Somodevilla/Staff/Getty Images News/Getty Images; pp. 30, 36, 71 Bettmann/Bettmann/Getty Images; p. 34 Dennis Nett/Syracuse.com; p. 42 Courtesy of the U.S. National Archives & Records Administration; p. 50 Keystone/Getty Images; p. 51 Spencer Platt/Getty Images; pp. 52–53, 66, 67 Courtesy of the National Archives Catalog; p. 55 Adam Fenster/Reuters/Newscom; p. 62 Hulton Archive/Getty Images; p. 64 Alex Wong/Getty Images; p. 73 AP Photo/SJ; p. 79 Joe Raedle/Getty Images; p. 80 Matt McClain/The Washington Post via Getty Images; p. 82 SAUL LOEB/AFP/Getty Images; pp. 84–85 Jessica Kourkounis/Getty Images; p. 86 Rob Kim/Getty Images; p. 87 Joseph Sohm/Shutterstock.com; p. 89 Nicole DiMella/Rosen Publishing.

About the Author

Nicole Horning is a feminist who has written a number of books for children. She was able to earn her bachelor's degree in English and master's degree in special education thanks to the women who fought for that right during the women's movement. She lives in Western New York and reads and writes in her free time.